COOKING

UNDER the ARCH

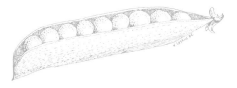

To the pioneer cooks of the West who knew how to cook on wood stoves, and raised their families on homegrown food.

COOKING

Cherished Recipes and
Gardening Tips from the Rigorous
High Country of Alberta's Chinook Zone

UNDER the ARCH

MILLARVILLE HORTICULTURAL CLUB

VICTORIA · VANCOUVER · CALGARY

TouchWood Editions

#108–17665 66A Avenue	PO Box 468
Surrey, BC V3S 2A7	Custer, WA
www.touchwoodeditions.com	98240-0468

LIBRARY AND ARCHIVES CANADA CATALOGUING IN PUBLICATION

Cooking under the arch : cherished recipes and gardening tips from the rigorous high
country of Alberta's Chinook Zone / Millarville Horticultural Club.

Includes index.

ISBN 978-1-894898-47-8

1. Cookery. 2. Gardening--Alberta. I. Millarville Horticultural Club.

TX714.C6565 2007   641.5   C2007-901411-9

LIBRARY OF CONGRESS CONTROL NUMBER: 2006940550

Edited by Corina Skavberg
Proofread by Marial Shea
Book design and layout by Jacqui Thomas
All cover and interior photographs by Pam Doyle,
except pages 1, 2, 4, 8, 26, 29, 30, 88, 154, 159, 160, 162, 163, 165,
which were supplied by the Millarville Horticultural Club
All drawings were supplied by the Millarville Horticultural Club

Printed and bound in Hong Kong

TouchWood Editions acknowledges the financial support for its publishing program from the
Government of Canada through the Book Publishing Industry Development Program (BPIDP),
Canada Council for the Arts, and the province of British Columbia through the British Columbia
Arts Council and the Book Publishing Tax Credit.

CONTENTS

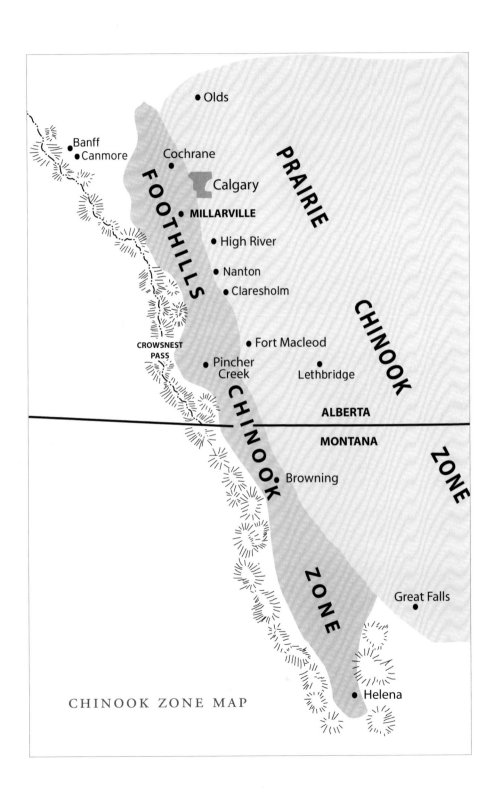

CHINOOK ZONE MAP

INTRODUCTION

THE SAME CREW FROM THE MILLARVILLE HORTICULTURAL CLUB WHO concocted the popular gardening book, *Gardening Under the Arch*, have followed up its new 2006 edition with this recipe book, which covers the sometimes overwhelming problem of what to do with all the produce from your garden.

Only recipes using fruit or vegetables from the garden or the wild have been included. All the recipes from the original editions (1982–1990) plus a whole lot of new mouth-watering favourites from the club members' kitchens appear here. Sections on wild fruits and wine have been added, as well as herbs in vinegar.

There are delectable salads, desserts to die for, shelves full of gleaming jars of jams, pickles, relishes and preserves, cooling drinks for hot summer days, as well as soups and oven-baked casseroles to fill your house with the aroma of a farm kitchen on a cold winter day. Also included are sections on using rosehips, and making sauerkraut and fruit leather. You will find many new ways to use the overload of zucchinis, including suggestions to use them as door stops or baseball bats!

The chapters on growing vegetables, herbs and fruit have found their way over from *Gardening Under the Arch* (2006 edition), so this recipe book can stand alone or be used along with the new edition of *Gardening Under the Arch*.

Enjoy the satisfaction of cooking with the products of your own garden, or from a trip to the Farmers' Market. These recipes will go a long way to help you get the recommended servings of fruit and vegetables per day for healthy living.

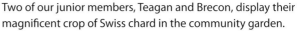

Two of our junior members, Teagan and Brecon, display their magnificent crop of Swiss chard in the community garden.

The First GARDENERS

ANNE VALE

"Adam was a gardener, and God who made him sees
That half a proper gardener's work is done upon his knees."
— RUDYARD KIPLING

THE EARLY PIONEER GARDENERS OF THE WEST HAD ONLY EXPERIENCE for a teacher. Those who were wise in the ways of Eastern Canada or Europe must have got a shock to discover that the frost-free days were somewhat erratic to say the least and their familiar planting-out dates did not apply. They had to find out the hard way whether they could grow tomatoes outdoors or get green beans to edible size.

Fresh vegetables came from your own garden or not at all. For the rural people store-bought food meant a long trip to town with the team and wagon and eventually the old truck or station wagon. The roads were poor, impassable when wet. Taking a passenger along was advisable, to open and close the many gates along the way to town. People stocked up on "staples" such as flour, sugar, coffee, tea, salt and canned food. Grocery stores were not able to obtain out-of-season fresh produce.

Keeping chickens and a milk cow or two were the rule for fresh milk, cream, butter and eggs. Ranchers would belong to a "beef ring" where each member in turn butchered a beef and distributed it fresh to other members, and so on.

The main problems with growing a vegetable garden were water availability, frost dates that curtailed the growing season to at most 90 frost-free days, and devastating hail that could be so severe as to strip every leaf off the garden. Fortunately, the long hours of sunlight made everything grow very fast. Local seed catalogues specialized in short-season varieties that did well here.

Gardeners became very resourceful and skilled at growing a vegetable crop. The magic seeding date was determined to be May 24th. July and

Patty Webb's Millarville garden in early summer: "Another season's promise in the ground."

August meant long hours spent shelling peas, slicing beans and canning. The root crops were stored in root cellars dug into a hillside. On a frigid winter day the lovely damp earthy smell of the vegetables in the root cellar was wonderful. The advent of home freezers in the 1950s meant less canning of tender fruits and vegetables and the end of the beef rings. If you didn't have room for a whole beef in your home freezer you rented a locker in town.

The garden was situated as close to available water as possible. Dugouts, sloughs, creeks or wells were common sources of water. High ground escaped many of the frosts but water was often a problem on a hilltop. Buckets, galvanized watering cans or sometimes the ultimate luxury of a gasoline pump and hose were used to irrigate the vegetables.

In spite of, or maybe because of all these difficulties, vegetable gardening became a proud and mostly successful art in isolated rural properties. Space being no object, the gardens were huge. The children were roped in to help weed and harvest. Usually the men folk cultivated and manured the site by team or tractor. Much sharing among neighbours went on, particularly with short-season crops like peas and beans.

This proud tradition still continues but on a much smaller scale than before, now that grocery stores are within easy reach on good roads and air freight brings fresh fruits and vegetables out of season. There still exists the pride of sitting down to an entirely homegrown meal.

An increasingly urban lifestyle means office-bound parents with no time or space to grow vegetables. Farmers' Markets are a great source of fresh vegetables now and Community Gardens in towns and cities rent growing plots to those whose thumbs still itch to grow their own garden.

Al Wells' VEGETABLE GARDEN

Al grows a huge vegetable garden back in the foothills where frost-free days are few. It is sheltered by stands of aspen at quite a high elevation. He rototills it with a tractor. He designs and makes his own labour-saving tools, which keep his garden free of weeds and his back free of aches. Al delights in sharing the produce of his garden with family and neighbours. He says he spends very little time maintaining his garden, but there is not a weed in sight.

MANY PEOPLE HESITATE TO HAVE A VEGETABLE GARDEN BECAUSE THE labour seems so excessive. This problem can be minimized by selecting proper tools and adopting good gardening methods. First-time gardeners should start with a small garden that has fertile soil with good water and air drainage. Frost and cold air travels to lower areas. Avoid areas where wind causes excessive drying and chilling of tender plants. Select an area that will give maximum sunshine. If there is a shallow amount of loam, more can be added. Don't try to plant every kind of vegetable available. Select early-maturing plants suitable for your climatic zone.

Till the soil as early in the spring as possible thus allowing the soil to warm up. This also kills freshly germinated weeds as well as roots from perennials. It is much easier to kill weed seedlings before planting your garden.

Garden seeders are available and can save a lot of work. However some people find it difficult to justify the expense of many elaborate garden tools. Some-times the cost of such tools can be reduced by

Al Wells with one of his handmade hoes.

sharing ownership with others.

I have found it an advantage not to plant everything at the same time. Planting some of each kind at different stages avoids loss from early frosts. Some vegetables such as lettuce, radishes, spinach and green onions mature and go to seed in a short time. Spreading out planting times gives a harvest when vegetables are at their best.

If you have a large area for a garden and have access to power garden implements you could summer fallow half the area each year thus reducing weed-killing work.

Ideally your vegetable garden should be located in a sheltered area where there is the most available sunlight and good drainage. A deep, rich soil that is neither too light nor too heavy is best for most vegetables. Well-rotted barnyard manure applied in the fall not only replenishes soil nutrients but improves soil texture as well. It can also be applied in the spring along with compost and should be worked into your garden either by digging with a spade or rototilling. Most gardeners in our area rototill two or three times in the spring and then rake the soil evenly in preparation for planting.

Squaring off your vegetable garden gives it a neat, tidy appearance and adds to the overall effect of your home gardens. To mark off your vegetable rows use a garden line, which can easily be made by tying an appropriate

Al claims that this extra-long-handled, lightweight hoe never gives him a backache.

length of strong twine to two stakes. Insert a stake at one end of your row, then run the twine the length of your row and insert your second stake at the other end, keeping the twine taut. Using the twine as your guide, hoe in your trench. Some gardeners recommend soaking each trench before planting your seed, as this may aid in faster germination. If possible run your rows in a north/south direction planting your shortest plants (such as carrots, radishes) on the east side of the garden. By arranging your garden in this manner your plants will receive full sun on three sides. If your garden is on a north or south slope, rows should run from east to west to retain moisture and prevent soil erosion.

It is a good idea to make a gardening notebook for yourself in which you can make annual notations about the types and varieties of vegetables you grew, the success you had, when and how you planted them, and so forth. Keeping a record of what you planted in each row of your garden (best done by numbering the rows) will assist you in crop rotation. This process involves moving your root, top and leaf crops to a different location in the garden every year, which greatly helps in disease prevention.

Competition from wildlife around Millarville necessitates this serious deer fencing.

Your garden soil needs to warm up before you plant most of your vegetable seeds. Cold soil can retard germination and growth. If you plan to mulch your garden to retain moisture and keep down weeds, wait until early July when the soil has had a chance to get warm. For mulch you can use peat moss, compost, lawn clippings, sawdust, hay, well-rotted barnyard manure or clean straw. To be effective it should be put on in a layer several inches thick. In the fall it is simply dug into the soil. Black plastic has also been used as a mulch by some gardeners. It not only conserves moisture and keeps down weeds, but it helps retain heat as well. Not everyone uses a mulch. It is something each gardener can experiment with to see if it is of advantage or not.

If you don't use one of the above mulches, hoe and rake after each rain or watering as soon as the soil is dry on top. This is known as dust mulching, which is just plain good farming. It will keep down the weeds and conserve moisture.

In most cases it is best to water your vegetable garden in the morning before the sun gets too hot. Try to avoid watering in the evening. A long, deep soaking is much better for your garden than frequent sprinklings, and if at all possible try to water with warmish water. Ponds and dugouts are a good source of water. It is a warmer temperature than well water and contains many organic nutrients. It is also naturally soft water, which is better for your plants. If soil and slope conditions permit we recommend trickle irrigation as the best method of watering.

Rain barrels to catch the rain water from roofs are a must. This is the best water for your plants, inside or out. Water conservation should be the main concern of every gardener. Surface watering rather than overhead sprinkling should be practiced where possible. The water table is having more holes drilled into it every day, and the supply below ground is not inexhaustible.

When it comes time to thin your vegetable rows (when seedlings are about 5 cm/2 in high) try to do so when the soil is damp. Be sure to firm your soil down well after thinning.

Recommended
VEGETABLES & VARIETIES

EVEN THOUGH WE LIVE IN AN AREA WHERE LATE AND EARLY FROSTS are a frustrating reality, a number of vegetables are grown successfully. These are listed below. All the varieties mentioned in this chapter have been tried and proven successful. However, bear in mind that new and improved hybrids are being developed all the time.

ASPARAGUS

This perennial vegetable takes four years from seed to be edible. Otherwise transplant two-year-old plants purchased from a nursery. Need deep, rich, well-prepared soil. Fertilize in April with a high-nitrogen fertilizer before growth starts. Needs lots of water. Harvest spears until the middle of June. Female plants bear berries so dig them up and throw them away as they don't produce as well as male plants.

Storage: Best to eat fresh. Asparagus enthusiasts have the water boiling before they even go out and cut it.

BEANS

Bush Type (Green) — *Blue Lake, Tendergreen, Dwarf Stringless*
Bush Type (Yellow) — *Golden Wax*

If the soil is warm you can sow beans in mid-May. Cover on cold nights. Very susceptible to frost. Don't cultivate or disturb beans when wet. In low-lying areas near the mountains it is difficult to grow beans due to frost. Harvest when beans break easily when snapped. In fall, after frost, cut off tops leaving roots in the ground, as they provide nitrogen.

Storage: Blanch and freeze; can.

Broad Beans — *Broad Windsor*

Plant early as they are slow growing. Quite hardy—will withstand spring frost. Pinch out growing top when plants are about 76 cm (30 in) high or when they have four or five sprays of flowers.

Storage: pick when young and tender to blanch and freeze.

Pole Beans — *Scarlet Runner*

Sensitive to frost—must be grown with protection either against a wall or fence. Attract hummingbirds.

Storage: Blanch and freeze.

BEETS

Tendersweet, Detroit Dark Red, Formanova, Early Wonder

When harvesting beets, twist tops off to prevent bleeding, rather than cutting. Beet greens are very high in vitamins. They can be harvested when young and cooked like spinach.

Storage: Pickle; cook and freeze.

BROCCOLI

Green Giant, Early Dividend, Goliath

Start indoors under lights or in the greenhouse in mid-April. Harden off in cold frame as early as possible. After transplanting in garden put a tin can from which both ends have been removed around seedling and push down

in soil about 5 cm (2 in). Remove before plant gets too big. This protects plant from wind and cutworms. Likes manure and well-watered rich soil. Harvest centre head first when still hard and green. Take 8–10 cm (3–4 in) of stem with flower head to produce high yield on side shoots.

Storage: Blanch and freeze.

BRUSSELS SPROUTS

Jade Cross, Bubbles

Same procedure as for broccoli. To hasten development, remove growing point when first sprouts are firm and remove lower leaves as sprouts form. Pick lower sprouts first. Require long, cool growing season. Harvest in late September.

Storage: Blanch and freeze.

CABBAGE

Red: *Red Acre, Royale* — use for pickling or salads.
Savoy: *Chieftain* — heavily wrinkled; easily digested.
Early: *Golden Acre, Early Marvel, Winner* — the first types to mature.
Mid-season: *Bonanza, Stonehead* — coleslaw or general purpose.

Late: *Danish Ballhead, Ultragreen, Safekeeper* — ready by fall. Best for sauerkraut and storage.

Golden Acre or Early Marvel have a small, firm, round head that matures in early July. Mid-season varieties such as Bonanza cabbage are a general purpose cabbage which can be used for coleslaw, etc. For storage purposes you should grow a late-season cabbage such as Danish Ballhead or Ultragreen. Red Cabbage is grown for salads and pickling as well as for its ornamental effect.

Storage: Blanch and freeze; store in cold room; pickle; make sauerkraut.

CARROTS

Amsterdam, Imperator, Touchon, Chantenay Types, Nantes types

Carrots like a sandy soil. Sow in garden in May. Water regularly—too much or too little water causes problems. To prevent green shoulders keep roots covered with soil. Plant in rows the width of your hoe and sprinkle seed randomly down the trench. This helps carrots to come up and although not much more space is used than if you planted a thin row, your yield is much greater. Harvest before heavy frost. Thin by using young carrots early in the season. Carrots for fall harvest must have room to grow.

Storage: Cut 1 cm (½ in) down from the crown to prevent growth and store in sand in cold room or in plastic bags in fridge; blanch and freeze; dry; pickle.

CAULIFLOWER
Early Snowball, Snow Crown
Same procedure as for broccoli. As soon as head becomes visible tie the leaves loosely up around the plant to prevent yellowing. Cauliflower requires a great deal of water so keep soil moist. Cold nights after planting out cause blind heads (no head at all). Plant out later than broccoli and cabbage.

Storage: Blanch and freeze at their prime; dry.

CELERY
Utah Green, Golden Self-Blanching
Start indoors under lights or in the greenhouse in mid-March. Plant in garden after danger of frost is past in 25-cm-deep (10-in) trench that is

filled in as celery grows. Needs lots of water and likes rich soil. Cold nights can cause bolting. Utah Green tolerates cold weather.

Storage: Blanch and freeze in unsalted water; dry.

CORN

Amazing Early Alberta, Head Start, Bowden Sweet

Likes lots of sun and rich, light loam. Must be sheltered from the wind. Needs constant water at silk stage. Plant three or four rows together with a distance of 1 m (3 ft) between rows for pollination. Most sweet corn will not germinate at soil temperatures under 10°C (50°F) so do not sow until your soil has warmed sufficiently, which may mean early June. Cover on cold nights after growing point comes up, for it is very sensitive to frost. Pick corn when silk on cobs is brown and dry and kernels are well formed. Corn seldom ripens here. The growing season is too short. Grow only early-ripening varieties.

Storage: Blanch and freeze on or off the cob; dry.

HORSERADISH

This indestructible perennial vegetable spreads rapidly so you should plant in a separate bed. Can harvest roots two years after planting. Harvest roots early.

Storage: Make into sauce.

KOHLRABI

Early Purple, Early White

Start indoors or sow seed directly in garden. Freezes well.

Storage: Blanch and freeze.

LEEKS

Large American Flag, Titan

Start the same way as onions and hill them as they grow.

Storage: Blanch and freeze.

LETTUCE

Head — *Iceberg, Great Lakes*
Butterhead — *Buttercrunch*
Cos — *Parris Island, Romulus*
Leaf — *Grand Rapids, Red Salad Bowl*

Sow seed thinly in early May. When 5 cm (2 in) high thin to 30 cm (12 in) apart. Thinnings may be transplanted. Water with trickle irrigation. Doesn't like hot weather. Can make successive plantings for continuous crop. Slugs can be a problem.

ONIONS

Sweet Spanish Utah Strain, Highlander
Red — *Red Burgermaster, Mars*

Start indoors or in the greenhouse—the later you plant them the hotter the flavour. As they grow, add more soil and feed instead of pricking out. Near the end of May, immerse flat in water so that seedlings can be easily pulled apart. Plant 10 cm (4 in) apart in an 8-cm-deep (3-in) trench. In August, remove soil from the top half of the onion and bend the tops over—this assists in the ripening process. At the first sign of frost remove onions from the garden. Set out in sunny location every day to dry on a screen for air circulation. When tops shrivel up they are dry. Hang in a dry place in old nylon stockings or net bags.

Storage: Dry; braid and hang in dry place; freeze (no need to blanch).

PARSNIPS

Improved Hollow Crown, Harris Model

Slow to germinate so sow radish seed with it to mark the row. Deep soil preparation is a must. Light frost improves the flavour. Leave some in the ground all winter and dig as soon as the soil thaws in the spring. Thin to give growing space.

Storage: Blanch and freeze; dry.

ALBERTA FRESH LOCAL
ONIONS
$1.99/
/Bunch

PEAS

Homesteader, Laxton's Progress, Green Arrow
Edible Pod Peas — Sugar Snap

As soon as your vegetable garden is dry enough to work, plant at least one row of peas. Plant varieties with different maturing dates for a continuous supply of fresh, young peas all summer. Often peas are planted two rows at a time, the rows being 15–20 cm (6–8 in) apart. In the space between the rows put in support posts every 1 m (3–4 ft) and stretch 2½-cm (1-in) chicken wire between them. Your peas will climb on and be supported by this wire and harvesting will be much easier. Peas like moist, rich earth so do not let your soil dry out. To avoid powdery mildew, remove old, unproductive plants by pruning at ground level. If your plants are attacked by powdery mildew be sure to remove and burn all the infected plants—don't put them in the compost heap. Roots of plants are left in the ground, as they are full of nitrogen.

Storage: Blanch and freeze; dry.

Kennebec, Norland, Netted Gem, Pontiac, Yukon Gold, All Blue

Potatoes help to clean the soil of weeds by competition, and they break up the soil. They use a lot of soil nutrients, which must be replenished the following year. They like a well-drained loam. Avoid letting the ground dry out or get too wet. Plant potatoes in rows 1 m (3 ft) apart with plants 46 cm (18 in) apart in the row. When they break through the soil, build the earth up around them. As they grow, continue to do this to support the stems and to keep the sun from the tubers. This process is called "hilling." It is best to harvest potatoes on an overcast day. Spread potatoes on a dry, flat surface to dry out, leaving some dirt on them. As soon as they are dry (a few hours) put in a humid, cool spot that is completely dark, for exposure to light causes their surface to turn green and poisonous. Potatoes keep well in bushel baskets in the cold room.

Storage: As above.

PUMPKIN

Spirit, Orange Smoothie

Grow the same as squash—needs lots of space and lots of heat.

Storage: On a shelf in cold room or root cellar. Will ripen in the basement.

RADISHES

Early Scarlet Globe, Cherry Belle, French Breakfast, White Icicle

May be planted every 10 days for continuous supply from early May on. Mix with rows of lettuce and carrots to assist in their germination. Otherwise plant in blocks 0.6–1 m (2–3 ft) square. Flea beetles can destroy radishes—to repel beetles plant mint with radishes or spray with catnip tea. Maggots can be controlled by spreading crushed eggshells over the soil surface around the plants. Grow best in cool weather so plant in spring.

Storage: Winter radish can be stored in cold room or root cellar.

RHUBARB

A perennial vegetable that prefers rich, well-drained, deeply worked soil and a sunny location. Plant roots just below the soil surface in May and allow to grow for two years before harvesting stalks. When seed stalks form, cut them off near the ground. To force a rhubarb plant for early eating encircle with bucket from which the bottom has been removed or else with several rubber tires. Remove later in the season. For jelly recipes calling for lemon juice, use rhubarb juice.

Storage: Jam; jelly; freeze; make juice, relish or chutneys; wine; dry; use in pies and other desserts.

RUTABAGA (SWEDE TURNIP)

Laurentian, Canadian Gem

These are grown for winter storage. Sow outdoors at the end of May. Must be thinned to 25 cm (10 in) apart. Water and cultivate regularly. Root maggots and flea beetles are a problem. In the fall when harvested, paint with a thin layer of melted paraffin wax after removing all maggot holes,

then store in the cold room, or put in plastic bags leaving the tops open, and store in the cold room.

Storage: As above. Also can blanch and freeze, or cook, mash and freeze; dry.

SPINACH

King of Denmark, Hybrid #7 F1, Leaf Beet Perpetual Spinach, Long Standing Bloomsdale

Sow seed in garden in early May. Water frequently. Likes well-rotted manure and rich soil. Keep cut so it keeps producing and doesn't bolt. Leaf Beet Perpetual Spinach will not bolt.

Storage: Blanch and freeze. Cook in larger quantities and freeze in family-size servings, undrained.

SQUASH

Zucchini Summer Squash — *Zucchini Select, Golden Dawn*

Start indoors in peat pots and transplant to warm, protected spot that has lots of sun, or start outdoors under hot caps. Likes well-rotted manure or manure tea. When fruit starts to develop pick flower off end of fruit and

"Bright lights" Swiss Chard

discard. Young fruit is generally best. Very susceptible to frost. Zucchini is the fastest growing squash. Hand pollinate by transferring pollen from male flower to female flower.

Storage: Pickle; dry; freeze; grate and freeze for later use in baking.

Use: Bread & Butter Pickles and Dills; can be used instead of cucumbers.

Summer Scallop Squash — *Starship (green), Sunny Delight (yellow)*

Grow as Above.

Vegetable Spaghetti Squash

Grow in cold frame.

Buttercup Squash — *Sweet Mama*

Grow in cold frame.

SWISS CHARD

Silver Giant, Ruby Red, Fordhook Giant, Bright Lights

Plant at the end of May. Water frequently. Both stems and leaves are edible well into fall.

Storage: Blanch and freeze; dill; make relish.

Brandywine, Ultra Girl, Beefmaster, Sweet Million,
Tumbler (hanging baskets)

Should be started indoors. Like rich, well-drained soil. Fertilize with manure tea or Tomato Food. Epsom salts are good to acidify the soil. Prune a number of the shoots from the axils of the leaves and in mid-summer pinch off any blossoms, as there is not time for them to produce fruit. You want to concentrate the plant's energy on developing and maturing existing fruit. Must be grown in a warm, sheltered spot or in a cold frame. The plastic device called "Wall Of Water" is good to protect young plants. To prevent blossom end rot, an even supply of water is essential. Tomatoes are pollinated by the wind, not bees. When planted in a greenhouse shake plant at midday to assure pollination and proper fruit formation. Variety maturity days mentioned in catalogues refer to the number of days from setting of blossom to the ripening of the fruit. Don't grow anything with a longer day length than 56 days, unless you have a greenhouse.

Storage: Blanch, peel, stew and freeze; purée raw in blender, put in containers (such as empty yogurt cups) and freeze; can; make juice; dry.

TURNIP (SUMMER)

Purple Top White Globe

Not a storage turnip. Same growing directions as Rutabaga.

HELPFUL HINTS

> Spinach can be sown in August as the small plants will live over winter and you will have greens in May.

> Peas can be sown in fall. They will come up in spring before the garden is ready to work. Cold nights don't hurt seedlings.

> When onion seedlings started inside reach 15 cm (6 in) in height cut back to 8 cm (3 in). When transplanting to garden, trim both roots and tops.

> To store carrots over winter, cut off 1 cm (½ in) down from the crown so they won't sprout and grow in storage, then choose from the following:

  • Store in layers separated by newspaper in styrofoam coolers with lid closed.

  • Store in cardboard boxes with lid closed.

  • Store in pails covered with plastic bags.

  • Store in moist sand or peat moss. Do not allow the mix to become too dry.

> When planting out cabbage family plants and onions, prune leaves back halfway, especially if the temperature is high. It cuts down on evaporation, prevents wilting and plant shock, and gives roots time to get established.

> Throw in a few radish seeds when you plant slow-germinating seeds like parsnips, parsley, carrots and asparagus seed. It helps you find the rows when doing your first weeding.

> When staking tomato plants tie the stalks to support stakes with panty-hose. This will not cut into the stems.

> When shopping for seeds, choose varieties that will mature within our short growing season. Seed catalogues, which give a lot of growing information, are helpful in this challenging area. The seeds from the suppliers listed below have done well for our members.

  • *Alberta Nurseries, Bow Seed* (Box 20, Bowden, AB T0M 0K0, 403-224-3544, www.gardenersweb.ca). This company has served Alberta well since 1922, specializing in short-season varieties.

  • *Stokes Seeds Limited* (Box 10, Thorold, ON L2V 5E9, 800-396-9238, www.stokeseeds.com). The Stokes catalogue contains a wealth of information for beginning gardeners. Details include how many seeds per packet, number of days to maturity and, for example, how much seed is required to grow 9 metres (approximately 30 feet) of carrots.

Outdoor SEED SOWING & TRANSPLANTING GUIDE

Although May 24 is used as a wide guideline for the date to sow seeds, in the area covered by our book frost may come at any time of the year and vary greatly from year to year. Some plants are able to take far more frost than others and the earlier the tough ones are set out or sown the greater use they will make of the extra days to make a good root system. The following timetable works pretty well.

WHEN THESE ARE IN FULL BLOOM	SOW THESE	PLANT OUT THESE
Buffalo beans	Lettuce Peas Sweet Peas Poppies	Onions Pansies
Saskatoons	Broad Beans Carrots Turnips Beets Spinach Calendula Clarkia	Petunias Snapdragons Cabbage Broccoli Potatoes
Lilac	Green Beans Corn Zinnias Squashes Tomatoes Salvia Dahlias	Marigolds Lobelia Nemesia Alyssum

> Danger times for frost are when the sky clears off after a rain, and at the full moon.

> Newspaper, paper or cloth makes a better frost protection than plastic.

> To protect broccoli from caterpillars, cover the new plants with a light-weight breathable cloth, such as Reemay, while the white butterflies are busy laying their eggs.

> Plant potatoes when the poplar trees are leafing out.

> Borage in the garden attracts bees, which will also pollinate peas and beans.

Betty Nelson's WEATHER DIARY

Betty Nelson, a lifetime Millarville gardener, kept a weather diary of which an excerpt is shown here. It gives a good illustration of the extremely variable frost-free dates over 11 years.

1970	Planted veg. garden 1st week May.	Good year, corn ready Aug. 12.	Fall frost Sept. 9.
1971	Planted veg. garden 1st week May.	Hard frost July 3.	Hard frost Sept. 14.
1972	Planted veg. garden 1st week May.	Cold spring & summer.	Hard frost Sept. 20.
1973	Planted veg. garden 1st week May.	Hot May. Frost June 10.	Hard frost Sept. 15.
1974	Planted veg. garden 1st week May.	Wet May, hot June.	Hard frost Sept. 1.
1975	Planted veg. garden 2nd week May.	Dry, late spring. Hail July 3.	Hard frost Sept. 3.
1976	Planted veg. garden 2nd week April.	1st half April hot & dry. Frost June 5 and 13.	Hard frost Sept. 8.
1977	Planted veg. garden 3rd week April.	Dry hot April. Snow mid-May.	Hard frost Sept. 27.
1978	Planted veg. garden 1st week May.	Light frost June 6.	Hard frost Sept. 15.
1979	Planted veg. garden 2nd week May.	Late, cold spring. Frost 1st week June.	Hard frost Sept. 29.
1980	Planted veg. garden 3rd week April.	Early spring, leaves out April 27.	Hard frost Sept. 25.

RAISED BED Gardening

PAM BERRIGAN

THE UNIQUENESS OF OUR CLIMATE AND THE LOCATION OF OUR ACRE-
age provided many challenges to our gardening experience. With gophers,
mice, moles, extreme wind and the occasional July snowstorm we knew a
conventional summer garden was not for us.

We built two 10-m-long (32-ft) x 1-m-wide (4-ft) x 81-cm-high (32-in)
raised beds that we could cover to extend our growing season. The boxes
were constructed out of 5 cm x 20 cm x 5 m (2 in x 8 in x 16 ft) rough
sawn planks and reinforced every 1 m (4 ft) with a two-by-four support
frame. We filled our boxes with screened loam and peat moss. We water the
boxes with soaker hoses that sit on top of the soil. This allows us to adjust
the hoses when needed and keeps the water below the leaves to conserve
water. We attached 2½-cm (1-in) PVC pipe over the boxes every 1 m (4 ft)
to form an arch support for the plastic cover (we used 6-mil vapor barrier).
We extended the plastic 1 m (4 ft) on each end so we could form a strong
seal on the ends of the boxes. The plastic was secured along one side of the
box with ribbon ties underneath to tie the plastic when not needed. We
used grosgrain ribbon, as it was the only thing we could untie when wet.

We plant our garden around May 15, which includes our tomato plants
(I start these from seed in February). I do plant the tomatoes about 15 cm
(6 in) deep to help combat the wind. We plant the rows close together to
reduce weeds and conserve heat and moisture. We then water it well and
cover it until the end of June. We open the ends to let the air pass on warm
days but always close them again at night until the cover comes off.

This gardening technique has served us well. Although we are continually
making adjustments we can successfully grow large pumpkins, corn, peppers and tomatoes as well as celery, peas, parsnips, beans and the usual
garden delights. On average we yield about 27 kg (60 lb) of tomatoes,
27 kg (60 lb) of potatoes, 7 kg (15 lb) of peas, 27 kg (60 lb) of carrots,
6–10 pumpkins and generous amounts of the other vegetables.

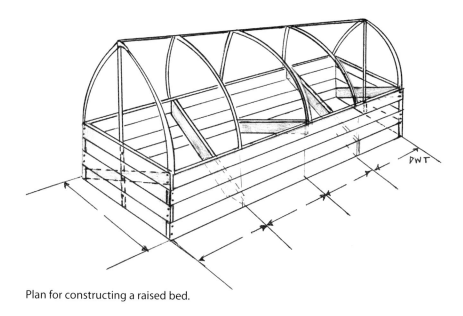

Plan for constructing a raised bed.

A luxurious crop of tender vegetables is exposed to mountain winds. A plastic cover can be pulled over hoops in bad weather.

HERBS

PATTY WEBB

SINCE I HAVE STARTED GROWING HERBS I HAVE FOUND IT A FASCINATING and rewarding part of gardening. Herbs can be grown along with your vegetables and flowers or you can plant them in a special spot of their own. Some of them can also be potted up and kept indoors to use during the winter. Most herbs grow well in a protected area in full sun.

I would like to share with you some of the experiences I have had growing and using herbs.

Pick leaves and flowers when flower buds are about half open—they have the most flavour and aroma at this stage. Also pick before noon, as soon as the sun has dried off the dew. Try not to crush them, as they will lose their fragrance, and do not gather more herbs than you can deal with

Linda Mackay's collection of herbs on her deck, which faces southeast on a hilltop west of Millarville.

quickly. It is, of course, better to use fresh herbs when possible but this is not always practical so we have to preserve them in some manner for future use.

AIR DRYING

Method 1

> all herbs should be dried in an airy, dry, darkened place
> cut herbs with a sharp knife
> tie into bunches and hang upside down
> should be dry in 1–2 weeks
> ready when brittle to touch

Method 2 (faster method)

> spread wet herbs on newspaper, cotton, cheesecloth or non-metallic mesh and arrange so air can circulate around them
> drying area should be warm and dry (can use food dryer)
> check herbs after about 12 hours—if they are brittle to touch they are ready to be stored

STORING

> strip leaves from stems
> do not crumble too much or they lose their flavour
> crumble or pulverize just before using for best flavour and aroma
> put into clean, airtight containers
> label and date containers (after a year discard old herbs)
> keep jars in dark part of the kitchen

FREEZING

> herbs are quickly and easily frozen
> gather herbs, wash and shake off any water
> put into plastic bags, label, date and freeze

Note: Flavour in dried herbs is more concentrated than in fresh or frozen, so you need a smaller amount. Usually ⅓ to ½ the amount you would use of fresh or frozen herbs.

Basil *(Ocimum basilicum)* — annual (frost tender)
> use fresh or dried
> wonderful flavour when used with all tomato dishes, eggs, bland vegetables, meat, chicken, fish and pasta dishes
> use fresh leaves in salads, and oil and vinegar dressings
> add to butter sauces for fish

Balm or Lemon Balm *(Melissa officinalis)* — annual
> use fresh or dried
> refreshing lemon flavour and aroma
> use fresh in fruit or vegetable salads
> season sauces, egg dishes, chicken and fish
> makes excellent tea
> use in potpourri
> use in herb baths

Borage *(Borago officinalis)* — annual
> use fresh for the cucumber-like flavour
> use young leaves in salads and cold drinks
> beautiful blue flowers can be used as a garnish in punches, iced drinks and in salads
> flowers can be sugared or candied to decorate cakes and other confections

Chamomile *(Matricaria chamomile)* — annual
> spreading habit
> makes a soothing tea for stress and digestion
> add fragrant flowers to potpourri

Chervil *(Anthriscus cerefolium)* — annual
> delicate parsley-like flavour with a hint of anise
> use fresh in soups or egg dishes
> sprinkle generously over chicken, pork, fish and shellfish
> add chopped leaves to butter sauces for vegetables

> especially delicious on carrots, peas and tomato dishes
> use to garnish and add to salads
> flavour does not withstand long cooking

Chives *(Allium schoenoprasum)* — perennial
> use fresh, frozen or dried
> mild onion flavour
> use as a seasoning in salads, baked potatoes, omelets and sauces
> the lavender flowers are also flavourful and can be added as a garnish

Garlic Chives *(Allium tuberosum)* — perennial
> not as hardy as regular chives
> use fresh
> use like regular chives where you want to enhance with garlic flavour
> can replace garlic in sauces and salads

Dill *(Anethum graveolens)* — annual
> use fresh or dried
> dill's pungent flavour is present in both seed heads and leaves (dill weed)
> the stronger dill flavour is more pronounced in the mature seed heads than the fine leaves
> use both leaves and seeds to flavour vinegar, cream cheese, dips, sauces, salads, salad dressing, eggs, poultry and, especially, fish
> dill weed makes an attractive garnish
> chewing dill seeds will freshen your breath

Garlic *(Allium sativum)* — annual
> use fresh or dried
> when garlic blooms, cut off the scapes before they set seed so all the energy goes to making bulbs
> harvest garlic in fall when foliage is yellow about halfway down
> replant garlic cloves in fall when planting tulips. Mulch if soil is very dry.
> store like onions

> for drying, peel and chop garlic bulbs and dry. Put dried pieces into blender and grind into powder.
> good in a variety of main dishes, dips and appetizers

Hyssop *(Hyssopus officinalis)* — perennial
> can be toxic in large quantities
> use fresh or dried
> leaves have a slightly bitter and light minty combination of flavours
> the unusual tang of flavour goes well in salads, soups and meats (especially lamb and stews)
> a little hyssop can be added to fruit and drinks
> hot hyssop tea is reported to help coughs

Marjoram *(Majorana hortensis)* — annual
> use fresh or dried
> a strong sage-like flavour
> used to season meats (makes duck, goose and pork seem less heavy)
> sprinkle over vegetables and legumes
> add fresh, finely chopped leaves to salads and salad dressings
> use sparingly, as it is a dominant herb

Mints *(Mentha species)* — aggressive perennial plant
> use fresh or dried
> use when cooking lamb
> makes excellent jelly and sauce
> use fresh leaves in salads, with early spring vegetables or in cool fruit drinks
> makes a refreshing tea (helps with digestion)
> plant in a contained area to curb its aggressive habit (for example, plant in a bottomless pail or bucket)

Nasturtium *(Tropaeolum majus)* — annual
> use fresh leaves and flowers

> peppery flavour similar to watercress
> good in salads and for garnishes
> add finely chopped leaves to cream cheese and whipped butter for unique spreads on sandwiches and canapes
> unripe seed pods can be pickled and used as a substitute for capers

Oregano *(Oregano heracleoticum)* — tender perennial*
> use fresh or dried
> sharper and spicier flavour than marjoram
> common ingredient in Spanish, Mexican and Italian dishes
> can be used in same dishes as marjoram

Parsley *(Petroslinum sativum)* — annual
> use fresh or dried
> there is practically no main dish it will not improve
> parsley accentuates the flavour of food without being dominant
> when used as a garnish it makes any dish look more tempting
> makes a good tea
> combines well with other herbs
> tones down the odour of strong vegetables like onions and garlic
> chew fresh leaves to freshen breath

Rosemary *(Rosmarinus officinalis)* — tender perennial
> keep over the winter as a houseplant in a sunny location
> use fresh or dried
> pungent savory taste
> pick young, tender leaves as soon as their aroma develops
> do not wash
> excellent in flavouring meats, fish and chicken dishes (especially good with lamb)
> use sparingly because the flavour can be dominating
> use in potpourri

Sage *(Salvia officinalis)* — tender perennial*
> use fresh or dried
> pungent aromatic flavour when dried
> fresh leaves are more delicate in flavour
> do not wash leaves
> good with all rich, fatty meats, poultry and fish (pork, goose, duck, mackerel)
> an important ingredient in stuffings
> makes a good spring tonic tea
> a strong herb, so use with care, tends to be bitter with long cooking

Summer Savory *(Satureja hortensis)* — annual and
Winter Savory *(Satureja montana)* — tender perennial
> both savorys have a robust flavour, though winter savory is stronger
> use dried or fresh (preferable)
> do not wash leaves
> very strong flavour, use sparingly
> good with all rich, fatty meats, and poultry
> best known for their use with all types of beans
> savorys not only give flavour but cut down on gas produced by beans
> put 2–3 fresh leaves in cooking water to eliminate the strong odours in cabbage and turnips
> a few sprigs in wine vinegar makes a tasty vinegar to use in French dressing

French Tarragon *(Artemisia dracunculus sativa)* — tender perennial*
> use fresh (can be preserved by holding in vinegar until needed)
> distinctive flavour
> important herb used in French cooking
> make tarragon vinegar by steeping the fresh herb in white wine vinegar. Use it to make French dressing.
> add to roast meats, poultry dishes and fish
> blend into light buttery sauces and serve with mild-flavoured vegetables
> will only grow from cuttings, not from seed. Even the seed reverts

to the common Russian type, which is a hardy perennial but has no taste.

Thyme *(Thymus vulgaris)* — perennial
> use fresh or dried
> do not wash
> has a very strong pungent flavour so use sparingly
> another important herb used in French cooking
> used in meats, poultry, fish, stuffings, egg and cheese dishes. Also good in salads, vegetables, soups and stews.
> helps in digestion of fatty foods
> use for tea
> use in potpourri
> use in bath for tired, aching muscles

Note: Tender perennials will not winter outdoors in this area.

HERB TEA

Whatever your taste buds desire in flavour will determine what herb or combination of herbs you will use for your herb tea. Just about every herb can be used for tea. All teas are made in the normal way. Just warm the pot, put in the herbs, pour in boiling water and allow to steep for 5–10 minutes. Use 5 mL (1 tsp) of dried herbs for each 250 mL (1 c) of water and one for the pot, or, if you use fresh herbs, use 15 mL (3 tsp) per 250 mL (1 c).

FRUIT
Apples, Currants and Raspberries

THERESA PATTERSON

APPLES

GROWING APPLES IN THIS REGION IS DEFINITELY A CHALLENGE! However, when you harvest the first pail of apples off your own trees you will decide it was really worth the effort.

There are a few tricks to achieving success with your orchard. The first is to choose varieties that are hardy enough to withstand our climate. The second is to plant them where they get some shelter from prevailing winds. A good snow cover is a help in keeping the roots frozen. Mulching after freeze-up with leaves and clippings helps, too. Be sure they are well watered-in late in the fall.

Now, what varieties can we grow? Crabapples are the hardiest. There are lovely flowering ones, such as Hopa and Royalty, grown mainly for their blooms; their apples are small and hard, but birds love them. Others such as Dolgo produce bigger apples good for jelly making.

Then there are applecrabs which are a cross between crabs and regular apples. Rescue is one of the best, a vigorous grower that produces when quite young.

If you want to try real apples here are a few to try:

Early (mid-August)
Heyer 12 — good cooking green apple, does not keep long
Norland — a new one in 1981. Has better keeping qualities than Heyer 12. Very reliable. Eat fresh or cook.
Battleford — worth a try
Mid-season
Prairie Magic — worth a try
Rescue Apple-Crab — very sweet. Extremely hardy.

CURRENTS

No garden is complete without a few currant bushes, red, white or black, or all three. The black ones have a strong pungent flavour, delicious in jam or jelly. Old-time remedies for colds recommend black currant juice in hot water, also good on a cold winter night even if you don't have a cold. Red and white currants make superb jelly. Their seediness does not make nice jam. Added to other fruits such as raspberries, gooseberries or crabapples they make jellies of excellent flavour.

It is best to provide your currant bushes with a permanent home where you can keep them free of weeds and grass. They will produce for many years. Whatever kind of soil you have it should be dug deeply and enriched with manure before planting. You can buy two-year-old plants or get some from neighbours by layering the lower branches or by taking cuttings.

Red and white currants are very susceptible to aphids and spider mites, which will denude your bushes of leaves if not treated. The crop will suffer as a result. Black currants do not seem to be affected as badly, perhaps because of their pungent odour.

It is important to prune currants to get a good crop of berries.

RASPBERRIES

Raspberries are a prolific fruit crop, well worth the little extra care they require to be successful in this chinook area. Since they bear fruit only on new canes from the previous year, the problem is how to bring those canes through the winter. Location also has a bearing on how well they will survive. An ideal location is an east-west row on the north side of a row of poplar trees. Leave at least 6 m (20 ft) of space between the trees and the raspberries to allow for cultivation. Also the trees will steal moisture from the raspberries. Avoid full sun and lack of protection.

Raspberries do well in black soil, or lighter if well manured and mulched with straw or hay. The mulch conserves moisture and keeps out weeds and grass. Do not cultivate too close to the row, as this encourages excessive suckering. Keep the row to no more than two plants in width. Remove extra suckers. It takes three or four years to establish a row that produces heavily.

They require ample amounts of water from flowering season right through fruiting. A plastic pipe with holes drilled every 13–15 cm (5–6 in) attached to a garden hose works well. Run the pipe down the middle of the row and leave it there all summer. Soak thoroughly as needed.

In late October or just before freeze-up bend the canes in a curve, using a light pole, until the tips touch the ground. Then place a board on the tips and shovel enough soil on it to hold the tips securely down. Be careful not to break them where they leave the ground. The snow will drift over them and protect them from the drying effect of the chinook winds. They do not require covering with straw or hay.

In the spring when the trees are beginning to leaf out, it is time to let the raspberries up. Uncover the tips and shake off the dirt. Now is the time to thin out the old canes that bore fruit last year. They will not have any new leaves coming. They look dry and lighter in colour than the new canes. Also thin out some of the new canes, leaving no more than four or five to a plant. The tops should also be cut back to no more than shoulder height. This encourages side shoots that produce fruit. Canes that grow 2 m (6–7 ft) high are hard to pick and they dry out and fall over. The canes need tying up now, too. Posts located every 3–4½ m (10–15 ft) down the row lend support. Strong baler twine run from post to post on each side of the row gives good support if cross ties are put in to separate the canes. Time spent in careful tying pays off at picking time.

Find a variety that thrives in your neighbourhood from a local source rather than ordering from elsewhere. Success is assured!

HELPFUL HINT

Grow currants next to raspberries. The birds prefer currants and will leave your raspberries alone.

Everbearing STRAWBERRIES

NORMA LYALL

I HAVE TRIED SIX KINDS OF STRAWBERRIES IN THE LAST EIGHT YEARS and find the everbearing is the best variety for our climate and soil. This variety does well in almost any kind of soil, the berries are red all the way through and you will have two crops of berries a year, in July and September, depending on the weather.

When planting strawberries you should have a place worked up the year before planting. You could work in natural fertilizer and old straw if you have clay soil. Try to kill all the weeds. If you don't have a place worked up the first year try your luck anyway and start another patch the next year from the runners that grew from this year's plants. Once you have a few strawberry plants you will always have them, for I don't think they would all winterkill.

As I have lots of garden space I plant my plants 60–75 cm (24–30 in) apart in the row and between the rows I leave 1 m (4 ft). For those who haven't got much space put plants 35 cm (14 in) apart in the row and 91 cm (36 in) between rows. I like to plant my strawberries so I can leave just two runners of each plant in between the mother plant. This saves transplanting. Once runners start you should go out every few days and place them where you want them to grow, cutting off the ones you don't want. You should only let about four to six runners grow from the mother plant each year. I let them bear fruit the first year as it is so much work to keep the flowers cut off. Remember not to hoe deeply around the plants because the roots spread out and are just below the surface. You should plant some new plants each year removing three- or four-year-old plants that are not doing very well.

Strawberries do best if there is a nice warm rain once a week and the weather is hot. Everything likes this kind of weather. Because of their shallow roots they should be kept moist, but don't allow standing water.

As strawberries catch all the weed seeds that blow around, such as dandelions and thistles, which thrive around the plants, they are very hard to manage. At times, looking after runners and weeds keeps one busy all summer, but the berries are worth the work you put into them. Also, when you have visitors all you need to do is take them out to the garden to the strawberry patch and tell them to eat as many as they like, then invite them in for tea. Sure handy when you haven't any cookies baked.

We have another problem in this part of the world, which is winterkill. This occurs when we have a mild winter and not much snow. One fall before freeze-up we covered the plants with old straw in which the weed seeds had sprouted and died. I left it to rot between the rows, which kept the moisture in and the weeds down and also helped to keep the dirt off the berries. When the trees start to bud you should take this straw off the plants a little each day and let the heat from the sun warm the plants. It might be late April or May when you uncover, as no two years are the same. This old straw prevented winterkill, however the dear little mice got into it and subsequently ate some of the strawberry plants off at the roots. Since then we have used old sawdust or old shavings as a winter cover, which has worked well. We uncover them the same way and leave the old shavings between the plants and the rows.

Strawberries must be planted with the crown of the plant level with the surface of the soil. If the crown is buried the plant will have difficulty growing and if the crown is above the surface the roots will dry out.

Recommended Strawberry Varieties

Everbearing—Produces a limited quantity over a long period—great for picking and eating fresh from the garden, or enough to make a dessert throughout the summer. *Fort Laramie*

June Bearing—Produces huge crop of big berries late June to early July. This is the one if you want to make jam. *Kent*

Day Neutral—These strawberries are affected by day length and will not bloom until the days start to shorten. Their fruit will extend your strawberry season right into September. *Tristar*

COMMUNITY Gardens

PEGGY GILLIS

IF YOU ARE A GARDENER AT HEART WITH LIMITED SPACE OR NO SPACE at all then a Community Garden may be the place for you. It must be clarified that public gardens with flowers, trees and shrubs may be referred to as community gardens, but are not the same as the focus of this article.

The real Community Garden contains plots for rent on a seasonal basis to provide those who are garden-space deprived the opportunity to grow vegetables and flowers. The garden can be the size of a residential lot or bigger, is fenced, has a water supply and hoses and a shed containing appropriate garden tools. Organic principles are encouraged. Our local garden has a communal bed of herbs for sharing. A bed or two is set aside for gardeners to use extra seed to grow a row for the local food bank.

The individual plots are in the form of a raised bed, contained by wooden sides and numbered for identification. The width allows the middle to be reached from either side and the length provides enough space to grow a good variety of plants. Most vegetables are suitable, with the exception of things like squash, which likes to sprawl, or plants taller than four feet, to prevent shading of adjacent plots. Intense planting works well and the amount of produce harvested is amazing. Flowers can be added for colour.

Garden users range in age from well-supervised children to seniors. To benefit the physically challenged there are beds double in height to reduce bending. There may even be a firm surface surrounding these plots for use by those with walkers or wheelchairs. These beds are usually close to the water and tool supply.

This gardening concept is a cooperative, encouraging renters within their abilities to be involved in managing the garden and in helping to keep common areas weeded and tidy. Working in the garden can be very spiritual, through sharing ideas and experiences and maybe relaxing a while on the garden bench, enjoying the fruits of your labours.

Why Are
FARMERS' MARKETS So Popular?

PAM VIPOND

HEIRLOOM TOMATOES, ORGANIC LAMB, WHOLE GRAIN BREAD, innovative wooden toys, giant dahlias, llama socks, jams just like grandma used to make and some she never heard of!

Why are people adding ranch-raised bison and elk to their menus? Why do those fresh tomatoes taste so darn real? When was that corn picked? How did you ever come up with that combination of tastes? These are just a few of the conversations overheard at a growing number of Farmers' Markets across Canada. At a time when food problems and concerns seem to get all the press, more and more people are going to their local market, getting to know the food producers, finding out how their food is grown and raised and enjoying the flavours, colours and delights of fresh, healthy food. Those other strawberries ripened in the truck on the way from California. People taste the difference. They are canning, jamming and creating when the real thing is in season. Corn roasts in late August! The Okanagan fruit is in! Ahh, good food!

Market vendors are a special group of people. They are experts and inventors, advertisers and entrepreneurs, educators and enthusiasts, achievers and administrators, all rolled into one. They are committed to providing quality products and informed service to their customers.

The people who choose to shop at Farmers' Markets are as varied as the products they purchase… veterans who know exactly what they want, show up 10 minutes early and disappear in a whirl of action, families and friends who make an event of the market, enjoying the food and companionship as much as the opportunity to stock up on their favorite treats. You'll find tourists, critics, gourmets and environmentalists, hungry folk and those who wished they hadn't had breakfast before they arrived.

A good market provides a sense of adventure and discovery as all these people mingle about and exchange tastes, tips and menus. They are a

The very popular Millarville Farmers' Market, held on Saturday mornings in summer, has become a meeting place for town and country and is a treasure trove of fresh produce and fine crafts.

perfect example of real people talking about and enjoying real food. Most vendors have samples available for you to try. They are proud of their unique tastes and it's an excellent way to taste new foods. There isn't a producer alive that isn't willing to tell you as much as you want to learn (and maybe more) about their products. What does ostrich taste like? How do you cook spaghetti squash? How is creamed honey made? What is the difference between Thai basil and lemon basil? These and a thousand other questions about good food are answered at every market. There are over 95 approved Farmers' Markets in Alberta alone and they feature a minimum "80% of vendors who make, bake, or grow their own products." The other 20% provide us with such treats as fresh fruits and vegetables from the Okanagan. The Millarville Market attracts thousands of people every Saturday all summer.

Take your time and enjoy the trip. Smell the fruit and the flowers. Or just let your good taste lead the way ... homemade perogies, spicy salsas, crunchy dill pickles, fresh mint, baby lettuce leaves and maybe even a few edible flowers for tonight's salad!

I still enjoy the thrill of driving to the market on a crisp morning before the sun comes up. It may seem a little early, or a little cold, but the sense of community and companionship that greets me each week as the market sets up never fails to warm me up. The people who choose to "savour time, rather than save time" make it all worthwhile. It all ties in, people mingle, smile and enjoy. We all share the seasons…from cold windy spring days, to the hot sun of midsummer, to the cool autumn days, when we pray for the snow to hold off. Perhaps the greatest sense of community is felt when it is cold, the rain is pelting down, the wind is rising, and only a few hearty folks arrive with their cloth shopping bags and enjoy hot chocolate or cappuccinos and commiserate with one another. Do not be surprised if you hear an impromptu weather-related sing-along or a group of vendors start doing jumping jacks to keep the circulation going to their toes. We know next week we'll be visiting those folks who serve fresh cold lemonade.

Pam Vipond is a happy vendor at the Millarville Farmers' Market. She creates fine foods made with edible flowers (Flowers As Food) and, yes, she has been heard "singing in the rain."

RECIPES

ASPARAGUS Soup

When asparagus is plentiful do try to make a batch or two to eat in the winter. It sure beats the canned kind.

Chop a quantity of asparagus in 2½-cm (1-in) pieces. Add a small chopped onion and barely cover with water. Cook gently until well done. Add salt and pepper to taste. Do not drain.
You can freeze at this stage in plastic containers.

To make soup:
Add 15 mL (1 tbsp) flour and 30 mL (2 tbsp) butter. Then add milk and some chopped parsley.
Optional—15 mL (1 tbsp) chopped cooked bacon is good.

To make Cauliflower or Broccoli Soup:
Can be made as above. Add 125 mL (½ c) Cheese Whiz at the soup stage and a shake of garlic powder. Serve hot, sprinkled with dried parsley.

BORSCHT Soup

750 g (1½ lb)	beets, peeled and chopped
1	medium onion, chopped
500 mL (2 c)	water
1	lemon, rind of
2	lemons, juice of
1 L (4 c)	milk
3	eggs
3	egg yolks
dash	Worcestershire sauce
15 mL (3 tsp)	sugar
to taste	salt and pepper
	sour cream

Boil the beets and onion in water until cooked. Simmer grated lemon rind and juice in a little water for a few minutes and strain into beets. Heat milk. Beat eggs and egg yolks and carefully add to the milk, stirring constantly. Do not boil. Add Worcestershire sauce, sugar, and salt and pepper to the egg mixture. Strain and combine with the beets. Chill and serve very cold with 15 mL (1 tbsp) of sour cream on each serving.

Granny Jean's BORSCHT

ARLENE JELFS

6	large potatoes, peeled
105 mL (7 tbsp)	butter
3	medium carrots, chopped
1	large beet
1½ L (6 c)	tomatoes (canned)
3	large onions, sliced
1	large head of cabbage
few	green onions, chopped
250 mL (1 c)	celery and leaves, diced
2	green peppers, chopped
125 mL (½ c)	chopped fresh dill
250 mL (1 c)	cream

In a large pot put 4 L (1 qt) water. Boil 3 potatoes in water. When done, remove and mash with 45 mL (3 tbsp) of the butter; set aside. Add carrots to water and salt to taste; cook. Add beet if desired. Add tomatoes. Chop remaining 3 potatoes and add to soup. Fry onions and ½ of cabbage, sliced fine, in remaining butter. Add mashed potatoes, green onions, celery and leaves, and the rest of the cabbage to the soup. Return to boil and cook vegetables. Lastly add fried onions and cabbage, green peppers, dill and cream. Season to taste. Heat thoroughly but do not boil hard as cream may curdle.

BUTTERNUT SQUASH Soup

2 medium-sized butternut squash

vegetable or chicken broth

1 onion, chopped

seasoning

curry powder

maple syrup

cream

Cut the squash in half, remove seeds, and bake in 180°C (350°F) oven on an oiled cookie sheet until tender. Remove flesh when cool and put in large saucepan with broth and the onion. Simmer until tender enough to blend. Add seasoning, curry powder and maple syrup to suit your taste and finish with a little cream.

(This can be made with pumpkin much the same.)

Cream of BROCCOLI Soup

50 mL (¼ c) margarine

50 mL (¼ c) chopped celery

1 small onion, finely chopped

75 mL (⅓ c) flour

4 OXO chicken bouillon cubes, crumbled

750 mL (3 c) boiling water

300 g (10 oz) broccoli

500 mL (2 c) milk

1 mL (¼ tsp) each nutmeg, pepper

garnish grated cheddar cheese

In large saucepan melt margarine and sauté celery and onion 3–4 minutes. Stir in flour. Cook 1–2 minutes. Dissolve OXO cubes in boiling water. Gradually whisk bouillon into flour mixture, bringing to a boil. Simmer over medium heat until slightly thickened. Remove from heat.

In food processor or blender, process half the broccoli. Chop remaining pieces. Add onion, celery and bouillon mixture to puréed broccoli. Process until smooth.

Return to saucepan. Add milk, spices and chopped broccoli. Reheat to serving temperature. Garnish with grated cheese if desired.

6 servings.

Golden CARROT SOUP #1

HELEN WILLY

This recipe was cut from a magazine at least 20 years ago and I have been using it regularly ever since. It can be dressed up in a fancy bowl for a special holiday like Thanksgiving or enjoyed as a family favourite anytime.

50 mL (¼ c)	butter
1	small onion, sliced
1¼ L (5 c)	water
625 mL (2½ c)	sliced carrots
50 mL (¼ c)	long grain rice
30 mL (2 tbsp)	chicken bouillon mix
1	small minced garlic clove (optional)
	salt and chopped parsley

Melt butter in medium saucepan. Sauté onion until tender. Add water, carrots, rice and bouillon mix. Bring to boil. Cover and simmer 25 minutes. Spoon vegetable mixture, part at a time, into blender container. Cover and blend until smooth. Add salt and parsley to taste.

Makes 4 servings.

Golden CARROT SOUP #2

AGNES WELLS

30 mL (2 tbsp)	butter or margarine
1 L (4 c)	sliced carrots
1	large onion, diced
1	large potato, diced
5 mL (1 tsp)	ground ginger
750 mL (3 c)	chicken stock, canned, homemade or from OXO powder
15 mL (1 tbsp)	parsley
15 mL (1 tbsp)	dill
15 mL (1 tbsp)	lemon juice
15 mL (1 tbsp)	orange juice
250 mL (1 c)	milk or half and half cereal cream

Sauté butter, carrots, onion and potato in large pot 5 minutes. Add ginger and chicken stock, parsley and dill. Simmer 15 or 20 minutes or until vegetables are tender. Add lemon juice and orange juice. Purée in blender. Return to pot and reheat gently. Gradually add milk or cereal cream. Enjoy.

Cream of CAULIFLOWER Soup

1	cauliflower
1 L (4 c)	milk
375 mL (1½ c)	vegetable stock or water
60 mL (4 tbsp)	butter
60 mL (4 tbsp)	plain flour
	salt and pepper
	chopped parsley

Cut cauliflower into florets and rinse in cold water. Combine the milk and stock or water and bring to boil. Add cauliflower and cook until tender. Press with liquid through strainer or purée in electric blender. In a large saucepan, melt butter and stir in flour. Cook for 2 minutes over low heat. Slowly pour into cauliflower mixture, stirring constantly, until smooth. Add salt and pepper to taste and cook for 10 minutes. Serve sprinkled with chopped parsley.

MINESTRONE

125 mL (4 oz)	salt pork or streaky bacon, diced
1	onion, sliced
2	large carrots, diced very thin
1	small head of celery
½	small cabbage, shredded
250 g (½ lb)	skinned tomatoes
2	leeks, sliced
250 mL (8 oz)	diced potatoes (optional)
1	clove garlic, crushed
1	small zucchini, sliced
2 L (4 pt)	stock or water (if using water used, add 125 mL/½ c chicken soup base)
125 mL (4 oz)	spaghetti, cooked separately, chopped (do not overcook)
1	small can tomato paste
125 mL (½ c)	finely chopped parsley
to taste	salt, pepper, oregano, thyme, a bay leaf, marjoram
125 mL (4 oz)	Parmesan cheese

Fry the bacon in a little oil (do not brown), then add onions, carrots and other vegetables except the parsley and zucchini. Sauté for 2 to 3 minutes. Add to boiling stock. Simmer for about 50 minutes. Add the zucchini, parsley and spaghetti, season to taste. Stir Parmesan cheese into the soup before serving. Leftover soup may be frozen. It reconstitutes very well. Other vegetables may be added as well.

LEEK & POTATO Soup

ANNE VALE

2 L (8 c)	chicken stock or bouillon
50 mL (¼ c)	butter
4	leeks
4 large or 8 medium	potatoes
to taste	salt and pepper
250 mL (1 c)	whipping cream

This is a delicious, quick and easy soup. Heat the chicken stock while the vegetables are cooking. Take a large, heavy frying pan and melt butter over low heat. Slice your leeks up to the green part, about ½ cm (¼ in) thick. Cook them gently in the butter until tender, taking care not to brown them. Slice the potatoes about ½ cm (¼ in) thick also and cook them slowly in the butter until tender.

Put the leeks and potatoes in the blender with enough broth to cover (hand blender is quicker and less messy) and blend. Add remaining broth, and salt and pepper to taste. Add a little whipping cream just before serving.

FRENCH Potato Soup (Potage Parmentier)

Hint: Add other vegetables such as broccoli, cabbage, green beans, corn and zucchini.
Make a big batch and freeze in cartons. Use ham, sausage or wieners in place of bacon.

6	medium potatoes
2	large carrots
2	onions
4	sticks celery
125 mL (½ c)	oil
4 L (1 gal)	beef stock or water and beef soup base
to taste	thyme, pepper
5–6	slices bacon
to taste	salt, parsley
	croutons

Peel potatoes and clean vegetables. Cut in fairly large pieces. Sauté them all first in oil for 2–3 minutes. Add the stock, thyme and pepper. Cook for about one hour. Sieve or put through the blender. Return to cooking pot. Cut bacon in small pieces and fry until crisp. Add fat and bacon to soup. Add the finely chopped parsley. Serve with croutons.

Serves 9–10.

POTATO Soup

THERESA PATTERSON

Dice 2 or 3 potatoes, 1 medium onion and a stalk of celery. Cook until soft in a small quantity of water. Add 30 mL (2 tbsp) each of flour and butter. Stir in well. Add a shake or two of garlic powder, salt and pepper, and 1 L (4 c) milk. Cook until thickened.

CREAMY Potato Soup

1	medium onion, chopped
10 mL (2 tsp)	curry powder
15 mL (1 tbsp)	butter or margarine
625 g (1¼ lb)	potatoes, peeled and diced
500 mL (2 c)	milk
10 mL (2 tsp)	chicken bouillon
250 g (½ lb)	spinach, trimmed and cut into strips
1 mL (¼ tsp)	salt
1 mL (¼ tsp)	pepper

Sauté onion and curry in butter for 10 minutes, stirring frequently. Add potatoes, milk, chicken bouillon and 500 mL (2 c) water. Over high heat, bring to boil. Reduce heat to low, cover and simmer 20 minutes until potatoes are tender. Purée in batches in blender until soup is smooth. Return soup to saucepan. Stir in spinach, salt and pepper. Cover and simmer 5 minutes until spinach wilts.

ROASTED Red Pepper & Tomato Soup

ANNE VALE

2	large sweet red peppers
	olive oil
12	large, very ripe tomatoes
1	onion
	chicken, beef or vegetable broth
to taste	basil, garlic, brown sugar
to taste	hot pepper sauce (optional)

Cut up red peppers, coat with olive oil and roast for a few minutes. Cut up tomatoes and onion, and simmer in the stock until tender. Put through the blender. Add seasoning. A touch of hot pepper sauce adds bite. Add roasted red peppers after blending.

CREAM OF TOMATO Soup

First, cut up and blend, skins and all, as many tomatoes as you have on hand to use up. Measure the quantity, then put on to heat slowly. Meanwhile, make an equal quantity of white sauce. Into the blended tomatoes, toss a few bits of celery leaves and some green onions, some chopped parsley and anything else found still growing in the herb patch. Add salt and pepper to taste. When sauce has thickened, let both mixtures cool to the same temperature, then slowly pour the red into the white, stirring gently. This will prevent curdling. You may also add a sprinkling of brown sugar and dash of soya sauce and good dollop of parmesan cheese. Even soup haters will ask for more of this one.

BEET Mold

37 mL (2½ tbsp)	gelatin
125 mL (½ c)	cold water
500 g (1 lb)	diced cooked beets
50 mL (¼ c)	vinegar
50 mL (¼ c)	lemon juice
150 mL (⅔ c)	sugar
5 mL (1 tsp)	salt
1 mL (¼ tsp)	black pepper
250 mL (1 c)	chopped celery
250 mL (1 c)	chopped cucumber
2	scallions, chopped
	shredded cabbage
	sour cream

Soak the gelatin in cold water for 5 minutes. Mix together the beets, vinegar, lemon juice, sugar, salt and pepper. Press through a sieve or purée in electric blender. Pour the beet mixture into a saucepan and heat to boiling. Stir in the gelatin until dissolved. Cool, then chill until partially set. Add chopped celery, cucumber and scallions. Mix thoroughly. Pour into an oiled mold and chill until set. Unmold onto a bed of shredded cabbage and garnish with sour cream.

BROCCOLI Salad with Red Onion

1	head broccoli, chopped
1	red onion, chopped
50 mL (¼ c)	sunflower seeds
50 mL (¼ c)	dried cranberries or raisins
	feta cheese
	Greek salad dressing, balsamic vinegar, spices

BROCCOLI SALAD with Grapes

1250 mL (5 c)	broccoli florets, break up small
250 mL (1 c)	each red and green grapes, cut in half
	crumbled bacon
	green onions, chopped
375 mL (1½ c)	toasted almonds

Combine all ingredients and mix well.

Dressing: Half Miracle Whip, half Creamy Lemon dressing.

BROCCOLI SALAD with Apple

375 mL (1½ c)	mayonnaise or Miracle Whip
22 mL (1½ tbsp)	cider vinegar
125 mL (½ c)	sugar
125 mL (½ c)	raisins
1000 mL (4 c)	raw broccoli florets
250 mL (1 c)	toasted sliced almonds
500 mL (2 c)	chopped green apple
250 g (½ lb)	bacon, diced, fried
125 mL (½ c)	sliced green onion
250 mL (1 c)	sliced celery

In medium bowl, stir together mayonnaise, vinegar, sugar and raisins. Refrigerate for 20 to 30 minutes to allow raisins to plump.

In large bowl, toss broccoli, almonds, green apple, bacon, green onion and celery. Add dressing and toss well. Chill 1 hour. Serve cold.

To toast nuts: spread on cookie sheet and bake at 190°C (375°F) for 5 to 8 minutes.

HELPFUL HINT

To remove caterpillars from harvested broccoli or cauliflower, soak in cold salty water for half an hour before cooking.

CABBAGE Salad

180 mL (¾ c)	sugar
5 mL (1 tsp)	salt
1	large cabbage, shredded finely
2	large onions, shredded or sliced finely
50 mL (¼ tsp)	sugar
10 mL (2 tsp)	dry mustard
250 mL (1 c)	white vinegar
180 mL (¾ c)	salad oil
15 mL (3 tsp)	celery seed

Combine 180 mL (¾ c) sugar with the salt. In large bowl, put vegetables in layers with sugar mixure and cover (I use gallon-size ice cream pails). Mix 50 mL (¼ c) sugar with dry mustard and add to the vinegar. Bring to boil. Add salad oil to hot vinegar mixture, cool slightly and pour over vegetables. Put either celery seed or a mixture of pickling spices in cloth bag and push down into salad. Cover and keep in fridge. Will keep for a month.

Hutterites Fred and Sarah Walters from the Cayley Colony have been vendors at the Millarville Farmers' Market since its beginning.

CARROT Salad

DRESSING

50 mL (¼ c)	vinegar
250 mL (1 c)	white sugar
75 mL (⅓ c)	salad oil
5 mL (1 tsp)	celery seed
1 can	tomato soup
2 mL (½ tsp)	dry mustard

SALAD

1 kg (2 lb)	carrots, peeled and sliced
1	large green pepper, sliced
250 mL (1 c)	thinly sliced red onion

Mix dressing ingredients together well.

Cook carrots for 10 minutes. Drain. Add green pepper and red onion. Add dressing and mix together. This salad will keep in the fridge for two weeks. Very tasty.

CARROT-RAISIN Salad

PAULA KROEKER

750–1000 mL (3–4 c)	finely grated carrots
125 mL (½ c)	sultana raisins
2–3	stalks celery, chopped
dash	salt
1 mL (¼ tsp)	cinnamon
75 mL (⅓ c)	mayonnaise (or salad dressing)
30 mL (2 tbsp)	sour cream or yogurt

Mix all ingredients well. Chill until serving time.

This is a delicious, moist salad that goes especially well with chicken or turkey.

CAULIFLOWER & Carrot Salad

375 g (¾ lb)	cauliflower
4	medium carrots
1	medium onion, chopped
5 mL (1 tsp)	sugar
150 mL (⅔ c)	mayonnaise
37 mL (2½ tbsp)	lemon juice
to taste	salt and pepper
	lettuce leaves

Chop the cauliflower into small pieces. Grate carrots and mix with cauliflower and onion. Blend together the sugar, mayonnaise and lemon juice with salt and pepper to taste. Pour over the cauliflower mixture and toss thoroughly. Serve on crisp lettuce leaves.

Paul Rishaug's vegetable garden

COMFREY Salad

250 mL (1 c)	pea sprouts or fresh peas
250 mL (1 c)	chopped comfrey
50 mL (¼ c)	chopped parsley or 15 mL (1 tbsp) dried parsley
125 mL (½ c)	grated carrot
50 mL (¼ c)	green onions

DRESSING

50 mL (¼ c)	oil
50 mL (¼ c)	lemon juice
50 mL (¼ c)	chopped fresh mint (15 mL/1 tbsp dried)
	kelp or spirulina

Combine salad ingredients in large bowl.

Mix dressing ingredients together, pour over salad and toss.

David Teskey's popular herb stand at the Millarville Farmers' Market.

CORN Salad

canned corn, drained

chopped green onions

chopped celery

cubed cheddar cheese

ground fresh pepper

Creamy Cucumber
dressing

Adjust amounts of ingredients until it looks right and you have enough. It tastes better if it can sit in the fridge overnight before serving.

LETTUCE & FRUIT Salad

1 kg (2 lb)	mixed lettuce leaves
125 mL (½ c)	thinly shredded red onion
	fruit

DRESSING

125 mL (½ c)	mayonnaise
50 mL (¼ c)	vinegar
125 mL (½ c)	sugar
125 mL (½ c)	milk or cream
15 mL (1 tbsp)	mustard
15 mL (1 tbsp)	poppy seeds

FRUIT
Use fresh peaches or mangoes (or canned or frozen) and/or mandarin oranges, canned and drained. Any fruit of your choice works. Pine nuts or slivered almonds can also be used. Combine with lettuce leaves.

DRESSING
Shake well and add to salad just before serving.

ORIENTAL Salad

THERESA PATTERSON

SALAD

125 mL (½ c)	toasted sliced almonds
½	small cabbage, shredded
85 g (3½ oz) pkg	Ichiban noodles, broken
30 mL (2 tbsp)	sesame seeds, roasted
1 pkg	bean sprouts (optional)
500 mL (2 c)	chopped green onions
500 mL (2 c)	chopped mushrooms
125 mL (½ c)	sunflower seeds
½ pkg	chow mein noodles

DRESSING

1	soup seasoning from noodles
125 mL (½ c)	vegetable oil
30–60 mL (2–4 tbsp)	soy sauce
45 mL (3 tbsp)	vinegar
15 mL (1 tbsp)	sugar
to taste	salt and pepper

Toss together salad ingredients. Combine dressing ingredients and toss with salad.

Refrigerate until needed. Toss gently again before serving. Serves 8–10. Any leftover salad can be stir-fried as a vegetable.

Spinach & STRAWBERRY Salad

HELEN WILLY

This salad is a light and healthy addition to any summer meal and is a delight when made with fresh spinach from the garden and fresh sweet strawberries.

spinach—enough for your crew

strawberries—same as above

DRESSING

75 mL (⅓ c)	white sugar
125 mL (½ c)	oil
125 mL (½ c)	white vinegar
30 mL (2 tbsp)	sesame seeds
1 mL (¼ tsp)	paprika
2 mL (½ tsp)	Worcestershire sauce
7 mL (1½ tsp)	minced onion

Mix your salad dressing in a jar and add to spinach. You may not need to add all the dressing. Add your sliced strawberries and enjoy.

SPINACH & Mushroom Salad

ANNE VALE

fresh young spinach leaves

clean white button mushrooms

bacon bits

This is delicious and very healthy. Quantities can vary according to circumstances. Don't go too heavy on the mushrooms. A vinegar-based fruit dressing such as Saskatoon or cranberry goes well with this salad.

MARINATED Tomatoes

5 mL (1 tsp)	curry
5 mL (1 tsp)	sugar
125 mL (½ c)	salad oil
50 mL (¼ c)	vinegar
1	crushed garlic clove
15 mL (1 tbsp)	parsley
to taste	salt and pepper
1 can	mushrooms, sliced
45 mL (3 tbsp)	green onions
5	large tomatoes, sliced
	lettuce leaves (for serving)

Combine marinade ingredients in jar and shake well. Pour over vegetables, and marinade for several hours. Serve on bed of lettuce in individual bowls or in large bowl.

ZUCCHINI Salad with Hard-Boiled Eggs

1 kg (2 lb)	zucchini
5 mL (1 tsp)	salt
3	egg yolks
5 mL (1 tsp)	dry mustard
125 mL (½ c)	oil
	lettuce
to taste	salt and pepper
45 mL (1½ oz)	cream cheese, cubed
3	hard-boiled eggs, sliced
125 mL (½ c)	wine vinegar

Wash zucchini, cut off ends, but do not pare. Slice thinly and sprinkle with salt. Let stand for ½ hour. Drain and put in bowl. Blend egg yolks, mustard and oil. Pour over zucchini and sprinkle with salt and pepper. Serve on lettuce, garnished with cheese and hard-boiled eggs. Pour vinegar over all.

ZUCCHINI Salad with Green Pepper

½ kg (1 lb)	zucchini
500 mL (2 c)	water
2 mL (½ tsp)	salt
1	clove garlic
125 mL (½ c)	chopped onion
125 mL (½ c)	chopped green pepper
125 mL (½ c)	celery
	French dressing

Cut zucchini in bite-sized pieces. Cook in boiling, salted water for 3 minutes. Remove from heat, let stand 2 minutes. Drain and chill. Rub cut garlic clove over inside of salad bowl. Place ingredients in bowl, toss with dressing.

Makes 6 servings.

Zucchini & KIDNEY BEAN Salad

45 mL (3 tbsp)	salad oil
3	medium zucchini, thinly sliced
2	medium onions, sliced
1	large green pepper, cut into 2.5 cm (1 in) pieces
1	vegetable bouillon cube or envelope
1 450-mL (15-oz) can	red kidney beans, drained
45 mL (3 tbsp)	white vinegar
10 mL (2 tsp)	sugar
10 mL (2 tsp)	salt
1 mL (¼ tsp)	pepper

Combine all ingredients and mix well.

Country comes to the city! A popular Calgary farmers' market.

ASPARAGUS–Fresh

ANNE VALE

*Very easy to grow in any climate. Takes 2 years from started roots to edible size,
4 years from seed. Very long-lived.*

Cut spears when they emerge from the ground in spring. Stop cutting by mid-
June so they can make foliage to feed the roots for next year. For best tasting
asparagus, get your water boiling before picking the spears and cook very briefly,
just a few minutes. When cooked they should still be slightly crunchy, not too
mushy. Serve with melted butter or sauce below. Try adding bacon bits: fry
2–3 slices bacon till crisp, crumble and add to cooked asparagus.

Almond Butter Sauce
Cook 50 mL (¼ c) slivered almonds in 50 mL (¼ c) butter over low heat till
golden brown, about 5 to 7 minutes, stirring constantly. Remove from heat, add
2 mL (½ tsp) salt, 15 mL (1 tbsp) lemon juice and pour over cooked asparagus.

Creamy GREEN BEANS

Soften one 90-mL (3-oz) package cream cheese. Blend in 15 mL (1 tbsp) milk,
1 mL (¼ tsp) celery seed, 1 mL (¼ tsp) salt. Add to cooked green beans and
heat through. Or substitute 2 mL (½ tsp) dill weed for the celery seed.

ROASTED Green Beans or Asparagus

LOUISE PATTERSON BRUNS

These are so yummy, I don't know why we didn't think of this years ago!

In a baking dish, pour 30 mL (2 tbsp) olive oil and 10 mL (2 tsp) balsamic
vinegar. Add ¼ kg (½ lb) long green beans or asparagus. Season with garlic, salt
and pepper, oregano. Toss. Cover and bake just until tender.

ELEGANT Green Beans

1 kg (4 c)	green beans
50 mL (¼ c)	chopped onion
45 mL (3 tbsp)	butter or margarine
30 mL (2 tbsp)	all-purpose flour
30 mL (2 tbsp)	sugar
30 mL (2 tbsp)	vinegar
50 mL (¼ c)	snipped parsley
250 mL (1 c)	dairy sour cream
3	slices bacon, cooked crisp

Cook and drain beans, saving 250 mL (1 c) liquid. Sauté onion in butter till soft. Stir in flour. Stir in bean liquid, sugar, vinegar and parsley. Cook, stirring constantly, till thickened. Add sour cream and pour over beans; heat through but do not boil. Crumble bacon over top.

Makes 6–8 servings.

Frozen GREEN BEANS

	green beens
TARRAGON BUTTER	
30 mL (2 tbsp)	soft butter
10 mL (2 tsp)	finely chopped tarragon
5 mL (1 tsp)	lemon juice
2 mL (½ tsp)	minced garlic
2 mL (½ tsp)	Dijon mustard

BEANS
Boil beans one minute. Cool. Put in freezer bag, cover with water, add enough salt for cooking, tie bag securely and freeze package. To serve, turn out of freezer bag into pot and put on stove at medium heat. Soon ice will melt and when it comes to a boil, remove and serve immediately. The taste and texture of the beans is excellent.

BUTTER
Mix; toss with green beans.

BAKED Beans

SHEILA NILES

½ kg (1 lb)	navy beans, or any white bean
1½ L (6 c)	water

Bring to a boil, and boil until beans are soft —¾ hour or so. Drain and reserve liquid.

ADD

10 mL (2 tsp)	salt
2 mL (½ tsp)	dry mustard
1	large minced onion
75 mL (⅓ c)	brown sugar
75 mL (⅓ c)	molasses
125 mL (½ c)	chili sauce or catsup
796 mL (28 oz)	can of tomatoes
½ kg (1 lb)	sliced fat bacon, or salt pork

Bake in 150°C (300°F) oven for 2–3 hours, adding more bean liquid when necessary.

I was a child in the Depression. This is my mother's recipe for baked beans. I never liked them as a child, I think mainly because we always had them on Friday night. Saturday was payday and go-to-the-market day and there was never anything else to eat by Friday.

Paul Rishaug's vegetable garden incorporates flowers.

BROAD Beans

ANNE VALE

Broad beans are easy to grow, frost proof, tasty and ornamental. They grow stiffly upright to about 60 cm (24 in) with showy white flowers. The long green pods are fur-lined and contain beans that are best when young. If they get tough, the outer skin of the bean can be removed with your thumbnail before cooking.

To cook: Shell the beans from the pod and boil until tender.

BROCCOLI Supreme

750 g (1½ lb)	broccoli
45 mL (3 tbsp)	butter
37 mL (2½ tbsp)	flour
125 mL (½ c)	sour cream
10 mL (2 tsp)	prepared horseradish
1 mL (¼ tsp)	thyme
to taste	salt, pepper

Trim broccoli and cook in boiling salted water until tender. Drain and reserve 125 mL (½ c) of the liquid. Melt butter in saucepan and stir in flour. Cook over low heat 1 minute. Slowly add reserved liquid, stirring constantly until thick and smooth. Add sour cream, horseradish, thyme, salt and pepper. Put broccoli on serving dish and pour sauce over. Serve immediately.

Brussels Sprouts POLONAISE

1 kg (2 lb)	Brussels sprouts
50 mL (¼ c)	butter
50 mL (¼ c)	fine dry bread crumbs
1	hard-cooked egg yolk, pressed through a fine sieve
30 mL (2 tbsp)	chopped parsley

Wash and trim sprouts and make 2 crosswise cuts in base of each. Cook uncovered in plenty of boiling salted water until just tender, 5–7 minutes. Drain and put in a hot serving dish. Heat butter in a small skillet until it begins to brown. Add bread crumbs and stir until lightly browned. Remove from heat. Add egg yolk and parsley and toss lightly with a fork. Sprinkle over sprouts and toss lightly again. Serve immediately.

Serves 6–8.

CARROTS with Honey

500 g (1 lb)	carrots
250 mL (1 c)	vegetable stock or water
to taste	salt
37 mL (2½ tbsp)	honey
20 mL (4 tsp)	butter

Peel carrots if necessary and cut into slices. Bring vegetable stock or water to boil and add carrots. Cover and simmer until carrots are tender. Drain. Season to taste with salt. Stir in honey and butter until both are melted and carrots are thoroughly coated.

SUNSHINE Carrots

7–8   carrots, sliced

Cook until tender, about 15 minutes. Drain. Combine in saucepan:

15 mL (1 tbsp)   white sugar

5 mL (1 tsp)   cornstarch

1 mL (¼ tsp)   ginger

Add: 50 mL (¼ c) orange juice and cook until it thickens, about 1 minute. Stir into juice mixture: 30 mL (2 tbsp) butter, and salt and pepper to taste. Pour sauce over hot carrots to coat evenly.

DANDELIONS: Early Spring Greens

Pick dandelion plants before flowers appear. Wash thoroughly. Take equal portions of bacon fat and vinegar. Season with salt and pepper and pour over greens just before serving.

LAMB'S-QUARTERS (or Pigweed)

Boil young pigweed until tender, then put in cold water and strain. Run through food chopper with some onion tops or whole onion. Cook in hot butter with salt and nutmeg. Garnish with hard-boiled egg.

LEEKS Au Gratin

1 kg (2 lb)	leeks
45 mL (3 tbsp)	butter
60 mL (4 tbsp)	flour
125 mL (½ c)	vegetable stock or water
250 mL (1 c)	milk
to taste	salt
to taste	nutmeg
250 mL (1 c)	grated cheese

Trim roots and damaged outer leaves. Quarter leeks and wash thoroughly in running water. Place in saucepan with about 125 mL (½ c) of water, cover and cook over medium heat until tender. Drain if necessary. Keep warm. Melt butter in saucepan and stir in flour. Cook over low heat for 1 minute. Slowly add vegetable stock or water, stirring constantly, until smooth. Blend in milk, continuing to stir until smooth and thick. Add salt and nutmeg to taste and half the cheese. Stir until cheese is melted. Butter baking dish and place leeks in it. Pour cheese sauce over leeks and sprinkle remaining cheese on top. Bake in 180°C (350°F) oven for ½ hour. Serve immediately.

Mashed PARSNIPS

500 g (1 lb)	parsnips
250 g (½ lb)	potatoes
to taste	salt
45 mL (3 tbsp)	butter
1	medium onion, chopped
	chopped parsley

Trim and peel parsnips and cut into thick slices. Peel potatoes and cut into chunks. Cook each separately in boiling salted water until tender. Mash separately, then mix together. Add salt to taste, and half the butter. Beat until smooth. Sauté onion in remaining butter until golden brown. Place parsnip mixture in serving dish and cover with onions. Sprinkle with chopped parsley and serve immediately.

BRAISED Parsnips & Carrots

LOUISE PATTERSON BRUNS

A sure way to get everyone to love those parsnips!

Slice parsnips and carrots on the diagonal, ½ cm (¼ in) thick. Pour a little olive oil in your nonstick or cast iron frying pan. Put in vegetables flat and season to taste with salt and pepper. Brown gently. Cover to let steam, turning to brown all sides. It is not necessary to add water if you watch them closely and keep the heat down.

SUGAR Snap Peas

DOROTHY JACKSON

Sugar snaps make great cocktail rolls. Make them a few hours ahead and store them, covered, in the refrigerator. Use squares of thinly sliced cheese, ham or other sandwich meats and roll the squares around strung, fresh sugar snaps. Skewer the rolls shut with toothpicks, garnish with olives, cocktail onions, radish slices, carrot curls, and anything else you can dream up that's colourful and tasty.

Another idea for a cocktail plate is to shell the peas and leave pods attached at one end. Stuff with cheese mixture that has had some of the shelled peas that have been mashed and added to it. Circle the stuffed pods around a chunk of cheese and serve with a dish of crackers.

Sugar snap peas make an interesting addition to any tossed salad. When making a vegetable gelatin salad, shell the peas and use in the salad. Unmold the salad and surround with the crisp pods filled with any favourite ricotta or cream cheese mixture.

Sugar snap peas can be added to sandwiches. The famous BLT sandwich (bacon, lettuce, tomato) can become BLP (bacon, lettuce, pea). Sugar snaps make a fabulous substitute for french fries to accompany hamburgers. Just string a handful of snap peas and serve them alongside your hamburger. Try dipping juicy, fresh sugar snaps into ketchup, mustard and/or mayonnaise.

SUGAR Snap Omelet

Prepare your favourite omelet recipe. When it is almost cooked, arrange cooked sugar snaps in centre. Fold omelet over and serve it hot.

Scalloped POTATOES & Carrots

30 mL (2 tbsp)	butter
30 mL (2 tbsp)	flour
5 mL (1 tsp)	salt
½ mL (⅛ tsp)	pepper
500 mL (2 c)	milk
1 L (4 c)	thinly sliced potatoes
250 mL (1c)	sliced carrots
250 mL (1c)	sliced onions

Melt butter, blend in flour and seasonings. Gradually add milk and cook until smooth and thick. To mixture, add potatoes, carrots, and onions, and bring to boil. Turn into greased baking dish. Cover and bake 30 minutes at 180°C (350°F). Remove cover and continue baking until potatoes are tender (about 25 minutes more).

SPEEDY Scalloped Potatoes

2	potatoes, peeled and sliced thin
1	onion, peeled and sliced thin
	salt
250 mL (1 c)	milk
15 mL (1 tbsp)	butter
30 mL (2 tbsp)	grated cheese or Cheez Whiz
to taste	salt and pepper

Put potatoes and onion in frying pan with 125 mL (½ c) water and a little salt and cook until barely tender, about 6 to 7 minutes. Add milk, butter, grated cheese or Cheez Whiz, and salt and pepper to taste. Thicken with a little flour and milk. This is a quick and tasty way to cook potatoes if in a hurry or unexpected company drops in.

Serves 2–3.

Frozen TOMATOES

Scald, peel, stew with salt and sugar to taste and place in freezer bag or other container and freeze.

Frozen TOMATO PURÉE

Freezing is a quick, easy and effective way to preserve tomatoes when they all come ripe at once. Just cut up some tomatoes that have a blemish or are over-ripe but still usable, put in blender, whiz them up, skins and all, pour into plastic picnic cups and freeze. When frozen you can easily pop them out of their cups and put them all in one big plastic bag in the deep freeze. Next time you have a recipe that calls for 250 mL (1 c) tomato purée, just get one measured frozen lump from bag and, hey, presto. No vitamins are lost by cooking with this method. Great in stews or Italian-type dishes.

ROASTED Tomatoes

THERESA PATTERSON

This is a great way to use up that bounty of tomatoes in the fall. These can be frozen in small amounts to use later, tossed with pasta, as a delicious hors d'oeuvres with cheese and crackers, or to give away at Christmas in your gift baskets. My friends clamour for them!

In a roasting pan, pour in:

30 mL (2 tbsp)	olive oil
15 mL (1 tbsp)	balsamic vinegar

Lay in a layer of tomatoes, cut in thick slices, or coarsely chopped. Sprinkle with:

	Italian herbs, oregano
	garlic, powdered or crushed
to taste	Montreal Steak Spice

Keep layering all of the above until you have 3 or 4 layers, or until you run out of tomatoes.

Roast for an hour or two, stirring gently away from the sides. The tomato juice will reduce and begin to caramelize. You will have the most wonderful aroma in the kitchen. Roast until tomatoes are thick and not too watery. Ambrosia!

Tomatoes VERTIS

8	large tomatoes
2	medium carrots
1	medium green pepper
1	medium onion
2	stalks celery
500 mL (2 c)	chopped spinach
22 mL (1½ tbsp)	parsley
60 mL (4 tbsp)	butter
1	egg, beaten
250 mL (1 c)	dried bread crumbs
125 mL (½ c)	milk
2 mL (½ tsp)	salt
to taste	black pepper
	grated cheese

Cut thin slice from top of tomatoes. Scoop out pulp. Chop all the vegetables coarsely and put through mincer. Melt butter, add vegetables and simmer until brown. Add egg, bread crumbs, milk, salt and pepper. Mix well, then fill the tomatoes. Sprinkle with grated cheese and put in buttered baking dish. Bake in 200°C (400°F) oven for about 20 minutes or until tomatoes are tender.

TURNIP Whip

15 mL (3 tsp)	instant chicken bouillon granules
1 kg (2 lb)	turnips (about 1.75 L/7 c)
30 mL (2 tbsp)	chopped onion
15 mL (1 tbsp)	butter or margarine
15 mL (1 tbsp)	parsley
2 mL (½ tsp)	sugar

In large saucepan, combine bouillon and 750 mL (3 c) water. Heat until granules dissolve and water is boiling. Add turnips (which have been peeled and cubed) and simmer until tender. Drain. In same saucepan, cook onion in butter. With electric mixer, whip turnips until fluffy. Mixture will not be smooth. Stir parsley, onion and sugar into turnips.

Vegetable CURRY

½ kg (1 lb)	green beans, cut into pieces
2	medium potatoes, peeled and diced
¼ kg (½ lb)	carrots, sliced
75 mL (⅓ c)	butter
10 mL (2 tsp)	cumin seeds
10 mL (2 tsp)	turmeric
5 mL (1 tsp)	ground coriander
2 mL (½ tsp)	cayenne
10 mL (2 tsp)	mustard seed
7 mL (1½ tsp)	salt
37 mL (2½ tbsp)	lemon juice
250 mL (1 c)	yogurt
250 mL (1 c)	fresh peas

Mix together green beans, potatoes and carrots and put into saucepan with enough water to just cover. Bring to boil. Reduce heat, cover and cook for 5 minutes. Remove from heat but do not drain. Heat butter in large saucepan. Add spices and gently cook for 2 minutes. Add vegetables with their liquid and the lemon juice. Mix well. Bring to boil, then add yogurt and peas. Reduce heat and cook over gentle heat for 30 minutes.

Vegetable SPAGHETTI SQUASH

Vegetable spaghetti is a novelty squash that looks like a plate of spaghetti after it has been cooked. It is rather stringy and coarse in texture compared to other squash. When raw, this squash has a delicious, nutty flavour and can be used shredded or diced in salads.

PREPARATION

Boiled—Cook the squash whole for about 30 minutes in boiling water. Cut in half. Scoop out the seeds. Pull the spaghetti-like pulp from the shell, and serve.

Baked—Cut in half and remove seeds. Bake in an uncovered pan at 180°C (350°F). If you wish, a few strips of bacon may be placed over the cut edges. This method takes about 1 hour. Or, use a little water in the pan, put the lid on and let the vegetables steam. The pulp should pull away from the shell and produce thin, spaghetti-like strands, ready to top with your favourite topping.

TOPPINGS

Be creative and don't be afraid to experiment. Here are a few suggestions:
  Salt, pepper and butter
  Canadian cheddar cheese sauce
  Parmesan cheese, sprinkled on top
  Tomato and meat sauce
  In a casserole as a substitute for pasta
  Serve cold with mayonnaise or French Dressing

STIR-FRIED Vegetables

Use any combination of fresh vegetables. Wash and prepare them all before you start. Slicing diagonally does not make them taste any different but is attractive. Use a variety of colours, textures and flavours, such as onions, carrots, edible pea pods, celery, asparagus, green beans, broccoli or cauliflower, cabbage, etc. Start with a hot wok or heavy saucepan. Add 50 mL (¼ c) oil. Begin with vegetables that take longest to cook. A little garlic and a thin slice of fresh ginger, fried first and discarded, adds flavour to oil. Add vegetables one kind at a time, stirring all the time. Do not overcook. The secret of stir-fried vegetables is to serve them tender-crisp. When all vegetables are in, add 125 mL (½ c) chicken stock, 30 mL (2 tbsp) soya sauce, salt and pepper to taste. Sprinkle with toasted sesame seeds if desired. Sauce may be thickened slightly with cornstarch if desired. Serve immediately.

ZUCCHINI

When choosing zucchini, try to pick small, young specimens that are firm. They can be baked, boiled, steamed, stuffed, scalloped, used in salads, main dishes, vegetables, quick breads, cakes etc. Your imagination is the limit with zucchini! Zucchini can also be frozen for later use in quick breads or casseroles.

ZUCCHINI Deluxe

3 large or 6 small	zucchini
1½ L (6 c)	fresh bread crumbs
50 mL (¼ c)	chopped onion
1	medium tomato, chopped
2 mL (½ tsp)	salt
1 mL (¼ tsp)	pepper
30 mL (2 tbsp)	butter, melted
250 g (½ lb)	processed cheese, cubed
50 mL (¼ c)	milk
6	slices cooked bacon, crumbled

Trim ends of zucchini. Cook, covered, in boiling water (salted) 5–8 minutes. Drain. Cut in half lengthwise. Scoop out centre of each and chop. Combine chopped zucchini, bread crumbs, onion, tomato, seasonings, butter; toss lightly. Fill each shell, place in shallow baking dish. Bake at 180°C (350°F) 25–30 minutes. Heat cheese and milk in saucepan over low heat, stirring until sauce is smooth. Add bacon, serve over zucchini.

Makes 6 servings.

ITALIAN Zucchini

50 mL (¼ c)	minced onion
50 mL (¼ c)	minced green pepper
30 mL (2 tbsp)	chopped parsley
625 g (1¼ lb)	zucchini, cut into 1 cm (½ in) pieces
500 mL (2 c)	chopped tomatoes
50 mL (¼ c)	fine, dry bread crumbs
180 mL (¾ c)	Italian salad dressing

Combine ingredients in order given, in 2 L (2 qt) casserole. Cover. Bake in 180°C (350°F) oven until zucchini is tender, about 1 hour. Stir once during baking.

Makes 6 servings.

Try dressing up your VEGETABLES

IDA WEGELIN

- Add some slivered almonds to your green beans.

- A mixture of broccoli, crumbled bacon, and mushrooms is tasty.

- A cream sauce with Cheese Whiz, or a couple of processed cheese slices added, goes nicely on cauliflower or Swiss chard.

- Try adding a few silver skin onions to your peas.

- In the spring when your potatoes are old try adding a sprig of fresh mint to them as you boil them.

- Bread crumbs browned in butter or margarine go nicely on parsnips, Swiss chard or chard greens.

- Add a tablespoon or two of finely chopped onions to your mashed potatoes.

- *Beets are fun to work with:*

   1. Make a glaze of 45 mL (3 tbsp) butter, 50 mL (¼ c) orange marmalade and 15 mL (1 tbsp) of orange juice. Heat in a skillet then pour over cooked beets, sliced or diced.

   2. Make an orange sauce of 15 mL (1 tbsp) butter, 15 mL (1 tbsp) flour, 45 mL (3 tbsp) orange juice, and 22 mL (1½ tbsp) sugar. Cook until thickened. Add to sliced or cubed beets.

   3. Just add orange juice to beets.

- Carrots are tasty in a cream sauce with a few small onions added.

- I like boiling my cabbage in milk to which I've added celery seed and a teaspoon or two of butter or margarine. Don't throw the milk out—it's good to drink.

- Don't forget to use spices on vegetables. For example, a little nutmeg or mace may be added to turnips or mixed vegetables. Dill, parsley or ginger goes nicely on carrots. (Grated fresh ginger may be used too.)

- Several other spices that could be sprinkled on your vegetables are basil, caraway seeds, tarragon, nutmeg, allspice, sesame seeds, thyme or oregano. Let your taste buds be your guide as you experiment.

Broccoli & Chicken CASSEROLE

Sauté 125 mL (½ c) chopped onion, 125 mL (½ c) chopped celery and 50 mL (¼ c) butter. Add ½ kg (1 lb) of cooked, drained broccoli to 250 mL (1 c) cooked rice. Heat 1 can mushroom soup with about 250 mL (1 c) Cheese Whiz. Heat until cheese is melted. Stir into mixture of celery, onion, broccoli and rice. Add 375 mL (1½ c) cooked chicken. Put into casserole. Top with slivered almonds. Cover and bake at 180°C (350°F) for 35–45 minutes.

CARROT TURNIP Bake

1	large turnip, peeled and cubed
3	large carrots, shredded
30 mL (2 tbsp)	butter
1	egg
30 mL (2 tbsp)	brown sugar
5 mL (1 tsp)	salt
dash	pepper
250 mL (1 c)	evaporated milk
250 mL (1 c)	cooked rice

Cook turnip, covered, in boiling water until tender. Drain. Cook carrots until almost tender. Drain. Whip turnip, butter, egg, brown sugar, salt and dash of pepper until fluffy. Stir in milk, rice and carrots. Turn into baking dish and bake uncovered 35–40 minutes at 180°C (350°F).

Serves 12.

LEEK & POTATO Casserole

1 kg (4 c)	sliced raw potatoes
430 mL (1¾ c)	milk
6 mL (1¼ tsp)	salt
2	large leeks (375 mL/1½ c)
50 mL (¼ c)	fresh bread crumbs
30 mL (2 tbsp)	melted butter

Put potatoes, milk and salt in saucepan. Cover and cook until slightly tender, about 10 minutes. Shake the pan often to prevent potatoes burning. Arrange potatoes and leeks layer by layer in casserole. Combine bread crumbs and butter and sprinkle on top. Bake uncovered for about 20 minutes.

Paul Rishaug in his wonderful garden.

TOMATO & CELERY Casserole

1 796-mL (28-oz) can	tomatoes
500 mL (2 c)	celery, cut in 1 cm (½ in) pieces
1	medium onion, cut fine
15 mL (1 tbsp)	flour
15 mL (1 tbsp)	sugar
5 mL (1 tsp)	salt
250 mL (1 c)	bread crumbs
45 mL (3 tbsp)	melted butter

Place vegetables in baking dish. Mix flour, sugar and salt and add to vegetables. Combine bread crumbs with melted butter and sprinkle on top of vegetables. Bake one hour at 160°C (325°F), uncovered.

SAUTÉED BEEF STEAK
with Fresh Vegetables (Stove Top)

120 g (4 oz)	top round or sirloin steak per serving
½	peeled carrot, cut in 1 cm (½ in) pieces
1	stick celery, cut in 1 cm (½ in) pieces
¼	head fresh cauliflower, cut in florets
1	head broccoli, cut in florets
1	very small clove fresh garlic
1	slice of fresh ginger
½	small green pepper, cut in 1 cm (½ in) pieces
3 or 4	fresh mushrooms, with stems
to taste	salt and pepper
	soya sauce
	cornstarch for thickening
3–4	green onions for garnish

Marinate the beef with 1 mL (¼ tsp) salt, 2 mL (½ tsp) sugar, 15 mL (1 tbsp) soya sauce, 5 mL (1 tsp) oil, 5 mL (1 tsp) cornstarch and 5 mL (1 tsp) brown sugar, for half an hour or longer.

Cook carrots 4–5 minutes and cool in cold water. Boil the rest of the vegetables, except mushrooms, green peppers and green onions, for 30–45 seconds. Remove and plunge into cold water and dry them when cold.

Heat the wok, add 10 mL (2 tsp) oil. Add garlic, brown and discard. Ginger can be added, browned and discarded. Add beef, sauté until 60–65% cooked. Remove.

Put all the vegetables in the wok and fry 2–3 minutes. Add 125–180 mL (½–¾ c) water or chicken stock, cover and bring to boil for 2 minutes. Taste and adjust the seasonings and thicken with cornstarch. Add beef and mix. Cut green onions and sprinkle over the dish when cooked.

Zucchini LASAGNA

THERESA PATTERSON

When zucchinis flourish in your garden and you are looking for alternative ways to use them other than as doorstops or baseball bats, try this lasagna, substituting zucchini for noodles. It is just as tasty.

½ kg (1 lb)	ground beef
1	clove garlic, crushed
15 mL (1 tbsp)	chopped parsley
15 mL (1 tbsp)	basil
5 mL (1 tsp)	salt
500 mL (2 c)	cooked tomatoes
2 180-mL (6-oz) cans	tomato paste
750 mL (3 c)	cream-style cottage cheese
2	beaten eggs
1 mL (¼ tsp)	salt
2 mL (½ tsp)	pepper
30 mL (2 tbsp)	chopped parsley
125 mL (½ c)	grated Parmesan cheese
2	medium zucchini
½ kg (1 lb)	Mozzarella cheese, sliced thin

Brown meat slowly; spoon off excess fat. Add next 6 ingredients to meat. Simmer, uncovered, till thick, about 30 minutes, stirring occasionally. Combine the cottage cheese with the eggs, salt, pepper, parsley and Parmesan cheese. Slice a layer of zucchini in the bottom of a 33 x 23 x 5 cm (13 x 9 x 2 in) baking dish; spread cottage cheese mixture over. Add half the Mozzarella cheese and half the meat mixture. Repeat layers. Bake in moderate oven (190°C/375°F) for 30 minutes. Let stand 10–15 minutes before cutting in squares.

Hint: A layer of chopped spinach may be added as well.

Makes 12 servings.

Zucchini RATATOUILLE

LOUISE PATTERSON BRUNS

These vegetables are straight from your garden, not dolled up with eggplant or mushrooms, though there is no law against these.

Cut in chunks into a baking dish: Zucchini, potatoes, carrots, onions, tomatoes. Drizzle with olive oil, fresh or dried oregano, garlic, salt and pepper. Cover and bake at 180°C (350°F) for 45 minutes. Top with cheddar or mozzarella, and parmesan. Bake uncovered a few minutes until melted.

BEET & CARROT Loaf Cake

BEAT TOGETHER

180 mL (¾ c)	salad oil
375 mL (1½ c)	sugar
3	egg yolks (reserve whites)
5 mL (1 tsp)	vanilla
45 mL (3 tbsp)	hot water

ADD SIFTED

500 mL (2 c)	flour
15 mL (3 tsp)	baking powder
1 mL (¼ tsp)	salt
5 mL (1 tsp)	cinnamon

THEN ADD

250 mL (1 c)	grated raw beets
250 mL (1 c)	grated raw carrots
125 mL (½ c)	coconut or walnuts or raisins

Fold in beaten egg whites, pour into greased angel cake pan or 2 loaf pans. Bake at 180°C (350°F), 50–60 minutes, or in loaf pans from 30–40 minutes.
(I like to put wax paper in bottom of pan.)

PRIZE-WINNING Carrot Cake

PATTY WEBB

A recipe of my Mom's that I have won many awards with at the Millarville Fair.

180 mL (¾ c)	seedless raisins
180 mL (¾ c)	grated carrot
250 mL (1 c)	chopped nuts
7 mL (1½ tsp)	baking soda
375 mL (1½ c)	boiling water
550 mL (2¼ c)	sifted all purpose flour
7 mL (1½ tsp)	cinnamon
2 mL (½ tsp)	nutmeg
1 mL (¼ tsp)	allspice
1 mL (¼ tsp)	salt
180 mL (¾ c)	butter or margarine
375 mL (1½ c)	white sugar
2	eggs, whole
2	egg yolks
7 mL (1½ tsp)	lemon juice
7 mL (1½ tsp)	vanilla

Preheat oven to 180°C (350°F). In medium bowl put raisins, carrots, nuts and baking soda. Stir in boiling water. Let cool for ½ hour. Sift together flour, spices and salt. In large bowl beat butter until creamy. Add sugar a little at a time, until light and fluffy. Add eggs and egg yolks, one at a time. Beat well. Add lemon juice and vanilla. Stir in flour mixture alternately with carrot mixture. Pour into prepared pans. Bake 25–30 minutes.

Carrot Cake with PINEAPPLE

SIFT TOGETHER

500 mL (2 c)	all purpose flour
10 mL (2 tsp)	baking powder
2 mL (½ tsp)	baking soda
10 mL (2 tsp)	cinnamon
5 mL (1 tsp)	salt

Beat 4 eggs. Gradually add 375 mL (1½ c) white sugar, beat until light and fluffy. Add 250 mL (1 c) cooking oil, blend. Add flour mixture. Add 500 mL (2 c) grated carrots and 1 can (398 mL/14 oz) crushed pineapple (drained). Bake in 3 layers or in large 36 x 28 x 5 cm (14 x 11 x 2 in) pan at 180°C (350°F) for 30–35 minutes for layers and 50–60 minutes for large pan.

FROSTING

Mix butter, icing sugar and pineapple juice to make icing.

The Bar U Ranch National Historic Site maintains a fine, old-style vegetable garden.

CHOCOLATE-ZUCCHINI Cake

625 mL (2½ c)	whole-wheat flour
125 mL (½ c)	toasted wheat germ
125 mL (½ c)	cocoa
12 mL (2½ tsp)	baking powder
7 mL (1½ tsp)	baking soda
5 mL (1 tsp) each	salt and cinnamon
180 mL (¾ c)	butter or margarine, softened
250 mL (1 c)	packed brown sugar
250 mL (1 c)	granulated sugar
3	eggs
10 mL (2 tsp)	vanilla
10 mL (2 tsp)	grated lemon peel
500 mL (2 c)	coarsely grated, unpeeled zucchini (2 large)
125 mL (½ c)	milk
250 mL (1 c)	chopped walnuts
250 mL (1 c)	raisins
LEMON GLAZE	(see recipe in method)

Stir together flour, wheat germ, cocoa, baking powder, soda, salt and cinnamon; set aside. In large mixing bowl, cream butter and sugars. Add eggs and beat until fluffy. With spoon, stir in vanilla, lemon peel and zucchini until well blended. Stir in milk alternately with flour mixture. Stir in walnuts and raisins. Turn into floured, greased 3-L (3-qt) fluted or plain tube pan (25 cm/10 in). Bake in preheated 190°C (375°F) oven 45 minutes or until pick inserted in centre comes out clean. Cool in pan 10 minutes then turn out on rack to cool completely. Drizzle with lemon glaze (below).

LEMON GLAZE
Beat 500 mL (2 c) confectioners' sugar, 5 mL (1 tsp) grated lemon peel (optional) and 45 mL (3 tbsp) lemon juice until smooth. If too thick to drizzle, thin with a little more juice.

Makes 12–16 servings.

Pineapple ZUCCHINI LOAF

3	eggs
430 mL (1¾ c)	sugar
250 mL (1 c)	oil
10 mL (2 tsp)	vanilla
430 mL (1¾ c)	grated, unpeeled zucchini
430 mL (1¾ c)	crushed pineapple (well drained)
750 mL (3 c)	flour
5 mL (1 tsp)	soda
1 mL (¼ tsp)	baking powder
5 mL (1 tsp)	salt
7 mL (1½ tsp)	cinnamon
3 mL (¾ tsp)	nutmeg
250 mL (1 c)	chopped nuts

Beat eggs until light and fluffy, add sugar and beat till blended. Stir in oil, vanilla, zucchini and pineapple. Sift together dry ingredients and stir into egg mixture along with nuts. Turn into 2 greased and floured loaf pans. Bake at 180°C (350°F) for 50–60 minutes.

RHUBARB Cake

125 mL (½ c)	shortening
500 mL (2 c)	sugar
1	egg, beaten
500 mL (2 c)	flour
5 mL (1 tsp)	baking soda
5 mL (1 tsp)	salt
250 mL (1 c)	sour milk
500 mL (2 c)	chopped rhubarb, floured
5 mL (1 tsp)	vanilla
2 mL (½ tsp)	cinnamon
50 mL (¼ tsp)	butter

Cream shortening and 375 mL (1½ c) of the sugar. Add egg and beat well. Sift together flour, soda and salt. Add alternately with milk or creamed mixture. Add rhubarb and vanilla, mix well. Pour into 23 x 33 cm (9 x 13 in) pan. Mix cinnamon, butter and remaining sugar until crumbly. Sprinkle over batter. Bake at 180°C (350°F) for 45 minutes.

STRAWBERRY or Raspberry Short Cake

Save a few whole berries for decoration.

250 mL (1 c)	flour
10 mL (2 tsp)	baking powder
15 mL (1 tbsp)	sugar
1	small egg
30 mL (2 tbsp)	corn oil
125 mL (½ c)	milk
375–500 mL (1½–2 c)	fresh fruit, sliced or crushed, with sugar to taste
	whipped cream

Sift dry ingredients together in a bowl. Beat together egg, oil and milk and add to sifted dry ingredients. Mix lightly. Bake in greased 20-cm (8-in) round pan 15–20 minutes at 200°C (400°F). Cool but don't allow to get cold. Turn out on plate. Split in half. Put half of the fruit on bottom half. Cover with whipped cream. Put other half of cake on top and cover with remaining fruit. Top with whipped cream and decorate with whole berries.

CARROT Pie

500 mL (2 c)	puréed cooked carrot
2	eggs
250 mL (1 c)	milk
50 mL (¼ c)	butter
125 mL (½ c)	brown sugar
2 mL (½ tsp)	nutmeg
2 mL (½ tsp)	cinnamon
½ mL (⅛ tsp)	ginger

Combine ingredients and pour into unbaked pie shell. Bake in preheated 190°C (375°F) oven for 45–50 minutes.

CRABAPPLE Pie

Line 23 cm (9 in) pie plate with pie crust and sprinkle with 10 broken soda crackers. Beat together 250 mL (1 c) sugar, 250 mL (1 c) crabapple pulp (left over from making jelly), 300 mL (1¼ c) water and 2 mL (½ tsp) cream of tartar. Pour into pie plate, dot with 15 mL (1 tbsp) butter, sprinkle with cinnamon and cover with top crust. Bake in 230°C (450°F) oven for 10 minutes, then reduce heat to 180°C (350°F) for 20–25 minutes until golden brown. Serve with hot custard poured over top.

ROSY Crabapple Pie

PATTY WEBB

My mother-in-law had a wonderful crabapple tree in her backyard that produced loads of rosy red crabapples (not sure of variety). My Mom and I would get together after picking several pails of crabapples and have a pie-making bee using this recipe. We would end up with about 25 pies in the freezer to enjoy all winter long.

1 23-cm (9-in)	pie shell, uncooked, and top for same
1½ L (6 c)	unpeeled crabapples (cored and thickly sliced)
5 mL (1 tsp)	vanilla
22 mL (1½ tbsp)	lemon juice
75 mL (⅓ c)	water
250 mL (1 c)	white sugar
15 mL (1 tbsp)	flour
1 mL (¼ tsp)	salt
22 mL (1½ tbsp)	butter

Roll out bottom pastry and fit into 23-cm (9-in) pie plate. In large bowl, combine thickly sliced crabapples with vanilla, lemon juice and water. In small bowl, combine sugar, flour, salt, and blend together. Add flour/sugar mixture to crabapples and mix thoroughly to coat all slices. Spoon crabapple mixture into pie shell. Dot with butter, top with pastry, and seal edges. Brush top with a little cream. Sprinkle lightly with sugar. Bake at 220°C (425°F) for 15 minutes. Reduce heat to 190°C (375°F) and continue baking for 35 minutes until crabapples are tender and crust is golden brown.

Foothills of the Eastern Slope

SASKATOON Pie

THERESA PATTERSON

750 mL (3 c)	fresh or frozen Saskatoons
375 mL (1½ c)	cold water
125 mL (½ c)	sugar
15 mL (1 tbsp)	lemon juice, more if needed
30 mL (2 tbsp)	cornstarch
1 23-cm (9-in)	pie shell, uncooked, and top for same

Put Saskatoons into saucepan with cold water and cook until tender. The secret of cooking Saskatoons is not to add sugar until they are cooked. Then add sugar, lemon juice and cornstarch dissolved in a little cold water. Cook until thick. If desired, put a layer of raspberries (fresh or frozen) or rhubarb or gooseberries or tart apple slices in the pie shell. Then pour Saskatoon sauce over and put the top on, sealing the edges with water. Bake at 190°C (375°F) until nicely browned. You may need more sugar if you add the layer of fruit in the bottom. Also, sprinkle the raw fruit layer with a little Minute Tapioca to absorb the extra juice.

CARROT Cookies

125 mL (½ c)	soft butter
375 mL (1½ c)	brown sugar
2	eggs
500 mL (2 c)	sifted all purpose flour
10 mL (2 tsp)	baking powder
2 mL (½ tsp)	soda
2 mL (½ tsp)	salt
5 mL (1 tsp)	nutmeg
500 mL (2 c)	quick cooking rolled oats
250 mL (1 c)	chopped dates
250 mL (1 c)	finely grated raw carrot

Preheat oven to 180°C (350°F). Grease cookie sheet. Beat butter, sugar and eggs together until fluffy. Sift flour, baking powder, soda, salt and nutmeg together into first mixture and stir to blend. Stir in rolled oats, dates and carrots. Drop by teaspoons onto prepared cookie sheet. Flatten slightly with fork and bake 12–15 minutes or until set and nicely browned.

RASPBERRY Slice

PATTY WEBB

I struggled with my raspberry patch for a number of years. I chose a variety suitable for the area, mulched, fertilized and watered it diligently, but it produced poorly. In the spring, I pondered the thought of doing away with the patch. While uncovering the canes, I decided to reconsider and muttered under my breath, "Either you produce this year or you are out of here!!" That summer I had the best crop ever. I was able to use my own raspberries for this recipe.

25-cm (10-in)   pan

BASE

125 mL (½ c)	brown sugar
375 mL (1½ c)	graham crumbs
75 mL (⅓ c)	melted butter
2 mL (½ tsp)	cinnamon

Mix together and save 125 mL (½ c) for the top. Press remainder in pan and set in fridge for a few minutes.

FILLING

225 g (8 oz)	cream cheese, softened
125 mL (½ c)	icing sugar
2 mL (½ tsp)	vanilla

Beat until soft and fluffy. Spread on wafer base.

1	small package raspberry Jello
250 mL (1 c)	boiling water
15 mL (1 tbsp)	lemon juice

Dissolve and stir in large bowl.

625 mL (2½ c)	frozen raspberries

Fold into Jello mixture. Pour over cream cheese mixture. Chill.

continued on following page …

235 mL (½ pt)	whipping cream
30 mL (2 tbsp)	icing sugar
2 mL (½ tsp)	vanilla

Whip and spread over chilled raspberry mixture. Sprinkle remaining crumbs on top. Chill for several hours before serving. Can be frozen up to 6 months.

GOOSEBERRY Fool

BERYL WEST

500 mL (2 c)	gooseberries, cleaned (cultivated varieties)
splash of	water
150 mL (⅔ cup)	brown sugar
250 mL (1 c)	whipping cream

Place gooseberries in a small saucepan. Add a splash of water to prevent them from sticking to the bottom of the pan. Add 75 mL (⅓ c) of the brown sugar and stir. Simmer on low/medium-low heat for 20–30 minutes or until very soft. Taste before the gooseberries finish cooking. Add more sugar to taste. The fool should be sweet and tart at the same time. I add 150 mL (⅔ c) of sugar in total. Set aside and cool to room temperature.

Whip the cream into slightly more stiff than soft peaks. Fold into the gooseberries. Place in individual glass dishes or a single dish to show off the lovely colour.

Terrific with ginger snaps on the side!

BLACK CURRANT Ice

375 mL (1½ c)   black currants

250 mL (1 c)   granulated sugar

15 mL (1 tbsp)   lemon juice

½ mL (⅛ tsp)   salt

3   egg whites

Place currants and 250 mL (1 c) water in a saucepan. Cover and bring to a boil. Reduce heat to low and simmer for 15 minutes or until mushy. Press through sieve and discard seeds and skins.

Meanwhile, combine sugar with 250 mL (1 c) water and boil for 5 minutes. Cool and combine with black currant juice (purée), lemon juice and salt. Pour into shallow cake pan and place in freezer.

When the outside is frozen (but inside still mushy) put into blender and blend until the ice crystals are broken down. Do not let mixture melt. Beat egg whites until stiff and fold gently into the semi-frozen purée.

Pack into containers, cover and freeze. Let soften in refrigerator about 20 minutes before serving.

RHUBARB Rolls

IRENE SMITH

This is a recipe that was given to me by my sister many years ago and is a favourite in our family.

250 mL (1 c)	flour
10 mL (2 tsp)	baking powder
1 mL (¼ tsp)	salt
30 mL (2 tbsp)	butter
	milk

Sift flour, baking powder and salt together and cut in butter. Add enough milk to make a soft dough. Roll out in a rectangle and spread with:

500 mL (2 c)	rhubarb, cut fine
125 mL (½ c)	sugar
5 mL (1 tsp)	cinnamon

Dot with butter. Roll up like jelly roll. Cut into 9 pieces and place in a greased 21 or 23 cm (8 or 9 in) pan.

Make syrup as follows:

180 mL (¾ c)	boiling water
180 mL (¾ c)	brown sugar
30 mL (2 tbsp)	butter

Pour over slices and bake at 200°C (400°F) for 25 minutes. Serve warm with cream.

RASPBERRY Mint Drink

Combine 250 mL (1 c) sugar, 250 mL (1 c) water and the grated rind of
2 lemons. Cook, stirring over low heat until sugar is dissolved. Boil 5 minutes.
Cool. Add 500 mL (2 c) crushed raspberries, 250 mL (1 c) lemon juice and
1 L (4 c) more of water. Serve in glass garnished with mint leaves.

Rhubarb SLUSH

HELEN WILLY

*This recipe was given to me by a friend and is a refreshing alternative to the ever-
popular rhubarb pie or rhubarb crisp. It's good with a shot of vodka too!*

750 mL (3 c)	fresh or frozen rhubarb
250 mL (1 c)	water
75 mL (⅓ c)	sugar
250 mL (1 c)	apple juice
1 can (180 mL/6 oz)	frozen pink lemonade concentrate (thawed)
1 bottle (2 L/2 qt)	lemon-lime soda

In a saucepan combine rhubarb,
water and sugar. Bring to boil.
Reduce heat and simmer 5 minutes or until rhubarb is tender.
Cool about 30 minutes.

Purée the mixture, half at a
time, in blender or food processor. Stir in juice and lemonade.
Pour into freezer container. Cover
and freeze until firm. Let stand
at room temperature for about
45 minutes before serving. For
individual serving, scoop 75 mL
(⅓ c) into glass. Fill with soda.
To serve group, place in punch
bowl. Add soda and stir. Serve
immediately.

Yields about 10–12 servings.

Rhubarb or CRABAPPLE JUICE

Wash and chop fruit. Fill large container with fruit (glass, plastic, pottery but not aluminum).

Cover with boiling water and let stand 12 to 24 hours. Pour juice off. Add 125 mL (½ c) sweetener, preferably honey, to each litre (quart) of juice. Heat to 80°C (180°F). Pour into hot sterilized jars and seal. Juice jars with rubber lined lids are ideal jars for this purpose. When ready to use, add 1½ times as much water. Rhubarb added to any other juice will take on the flavour of that juice.

SMOOTHIES

JEREMY KROEKER

Mix in blender after each ingredient:

8–9 ice cubes, or 250 mL (1 c)	crushed ice
500 mL (2 c)	fresh or frozen fruit (any combination of strawberries, raspberries, Saskatoons, blueberries, peaches, bananas, pineapple, kiwis, mangoes, or other fruit)
250 mL (1 c)	ice cream, any flavour
375 mL (1½ c)	milk
125 mL (½ c)	yogurt, any flavour

First crush ice in blender or add pre-crushed ice. Next, add frozen (or partially thawed) fruit. Then add ice cream and milk at same time. Then add fresh fruit. Last, add yogurt. Blend until smooth. This amount is good for 2–3 people.

SUNSHINE Iced Tea

ANNE VALE

Take a large, clear water jug. Fill with cold water, add 2 or more tea bags of your favourite blend of tea. Stand it in the summer sun all day to steep. Chill in the fridge until icy cold and serve with floating borage flowers on top.

Paul Rishaug, rancher, chicken fancier, gardener and award-winning flower arranger, with two prize roosters.

WINE-MAKING From Native Fruits

LOUISE PATTERSON BRUNS

Wine making requires some basic equipment that is readily available at wine stores. You will need a large primary fermentor, a Hydrometer to check specific gravity, a floating thermometer, a 23 L (6 gal) glass carboy for large batch or wine kit, a gallon jug for a small batch, an airlock, a siphon, and a long stirring spoon. Don't forget bottles and corks for later.

HELPFUL HINT

When picking wild fruit, take plenty of insect repellent and watch out for four-legged pickers with fur coats!

Saskatoon WINE

After trying many methods of wine-making, including using whole fruit that floated to the top and separated into fruit skins and pectin, I have decided that it is much easier to extract the juice from the berries using a steam juicer. The resulting juice is clear and pure and heat-treated, so it doesn't harbour strange bacteria, and I think the product is more reliable and predictable.

8 L (2 gal)	Saskatoon juice
2 L (½ gal)	dark Welch's grape juice
4.5 kg (20 c)	sugar
10 mL (2 tsp)	acid blend
2 mL (½ tsp)	tannin powder
10 mL (2 tsp)	pectic enzyme
5 mL (1 tsp)	yeast energizer
	warm water to 23 L (6 gal)
1 pkg	wine yeast

Starting specific gravity (S.G.) 1070 to 1080. This will yield a dry wine 11% alcohol. If too low, add sugar; if too high, add water.

Check S.G. every day and keep a record. When S.G. falls to 1020, rack to clean carboy and stop with an airlock filled with water.

When S.G. reaches 996, rack again, leaving sediment behind. You may add 5 mL (1 tsp) potassium sorbate at this point to kill the yeast. Stir periodically for 3 days to dispel the carbon dioxide. Let the wine bulk age in carboy for 6–9 months, then bottle. Filtering will improve the clarity of the wine and remove stray yeasts so your wine won't pop the corks.

APPLE-RASPBERRY Wine

Our Apple-Raspberry Wine has turned out to be a favourite because of its delicate flavours and beautiful colour. Using the method of page 110, try these juices.

8 L (2 gal)	apple juice (we use our Parkland and Patterson apples)
2½ L (10½ c)	raspberry juice
4.5 kg (20 c)	sugar
10 mL (2 tsp)	yeast energizer
12 mL (2½ tsp)	pectic enzyme
5	campden tablets, crushed
1 mL (¼ tsp)	tannin powder
	warm water to 23 L (6 gal)
1 pkg	wine yeast

Starting S.G. 1070–1080
Proceed as previous page for Saskatoon Wine recipe.

23 L (6 gal) yields 30 bottles of wine, which is a pretty good payoff for a few pails of fruit!

BLACK CURRANT Wine

This wine has turned out to be one of our favourites, a rich, dark wine, and not as strong tasting as you might imagine.

4 L (1 gal)	black currant juice
2 L (½ gal)	dark grape juice
5 kg (22 cups)	sugar
12 mL (2½ tsp)	pectic enzyme
5	campden tablets
	water to 23 L (6 gal)
1 pkg	wine yeast

Starting S.G. 1070
Proceed as previous page for Saskatoon Wine recipe.

If the fermentation does not start in a day or so, take out 500 mL (2 c) juice, dilute with 250 mL (1 c) water, add a new package of yeast in a large bowl, and cover with a plate. Every few hours add another cup of juice, until bowl is full of active wine. Then pour back into fermentor.

DANDELION Wine

Making Dandelion Wine is not for the faint of heart, for it is quite tedious, and a labour of love. You must gather the flowers in the spring when they are at their peak, and from a meadow with no dust from the road or any insecticide or herbicide spray. The petals must be plucked away from the green sepals and stems so that no green is left, which is bitter. The flowers have a delightful sweet flowery flavour. Even the wine, when finished, has the smell and taste of spring.

To make 4 L (1 gal) of wine, collect 1 L (4 c) of dandelion petals, no green

1 kg (4 c)	sugar
500 mL (2 c)	white grape juice (Welch's or other store brand)
1	campden tablet, crushed
	filtered water to 4 L (1 gal)

Starting S.G. 1070 to 1080.

Temperature 25–27°C (77–80°F)

1 pkg	wine yeast, sprinkled on surface

Let ferment in a warm place 25–27°C (77–80°F) for 5 to 7 days.

When S.G. is 1020, rack to a gallon jug and stop with an airlock filled with water. Let finish to S.G. 996. Rack again to clean gallon jug. Top up with water or white wine if necessary. Let age for 6–12 months. Bottle and cork.

Yield 6 bottles.

Christ Church, Millarville, at Flower Festival time in 2006.

GROG (Hot Mulled Wine)

While we're on the subject of wine, why not try some hot grog. On a winter's night, after skiing or tobogganing, or when you need a little treat, try this:

Pour some dry wine into a small mug, about half full. Add:

5–10 mL (1–2 tsp)	brown sugar or honey
dash	cloves and nutmeg
1	cinnamon stick
	top up with black tea or apple juice

In olden days, they would heat the grog with a poker from the fire plunged into the mug, but now we use the microwave. Mmmm…

CHOKECHERRY Wine

MARLENE LAMONTAGNE

5½ L (5 qt)	chokecherries
19 L (5 gal)	water
6½ kg (14 lb)	sugar
1	yeast cake

Boil cherries in water for 15 minutes, mash berries and strain through cheesecloth into large cooking pot. Add sugar to strained juice, mix well, bring to boil and then simmer for 30 minutes. Allow to cool to room temperature, add yeast, and let stand for 5 days before straining into 5-gallon crock. Let stand 2 weeks, then bottle or cork tight and leave for 3 months. If bottled in jugs, wine may be placed in smaller bottles at this time.
** *Important: Do not use metal utensils once the yeast has been added to juice.*

HERB Oils & Vinegars

DAVID TESKEY

MY FIRST RECOLLECTION OF HERBS WAS IN MY EARLY CHILDHOOD. As my family were great gardeners, they passed on things in a quiet way with purpose. Instilling in children the love of growing your own garden and its benefits was part of good parenting. My mother, who cooked a huge Sunday dinner and hosted the relatives, would say, "Run to the garden and get me a handful of mint, we're having fresh peas and potatoes." We didn't have money but we feasted royally on our garden and small farm. That was my first memory of herbs. We grew chives, parsley, thyme, summer savory and other common herbs. Dill for pickles. As I grew older I became more interested in the Mediterranean type herbs. Parsley, sage, rosemary, thyme, basils of all sorts. These all combined to make Sunday dinner smell so good.

I guess for me the smell of these herbs triggered the desire to cook and eat. As I began combining herbs in my cooking, I noticed a change in my family's eating habits. Everything tasted so good there were no leftovers. Add herbs to ordinary food and it catches people's attention.

I grow my herbs in a greenhouse on benches at counter height. These raised beds save on back-breaking weeding and watering. They are then right there at your fingertips ready to pick. Also they are at a good height to inspect for pesky bugs. I never use insecticides. Find a biological enemy for what's there and it works well. Ladybugs are my friends. They love aphids.

The beds have 16 centimetres (6 inches) of rich humous soil combined with peat moss and perlite. Five centimetres (two inches) of drainage rock under the soil and holes in the benches drain well onto the ground below. I don't heat the greenhouse all summer but it does get quite "Mediterranean" in the summer with the doors wide open. As I live in the foothills, I have come out in the early morning to find a deer just coming out, having dined on some of my finest rosemary and other tasty browsing.

Again, it's the smell. With 18 herbs all competing for the best of smells, how can they resist sampling?

As these herbs mature, they are cut and I dry them on racks in a darkened building with fans circulating the air. I turn them and inspect them daily to see they are not mildewing. In a few days they dry and the leaves can be stripped into large stainless steel bowls. Be sure to label when cutting. It's easy to get mixed up when they are dry.

Once they are dry I bottle them into nice big glass jars and store them in a cool dark place. You now have an inventory of basic herbs to play with.

The fun begins when you start cooking.

GENERAL DIRECTIONS
for Making Wine Vinegar

LOUISE PATTERSON BRUNS

AFTER MAKING MANY BATCHES OF WINE, IT MAY OCCUR TO YOU TO make some wine vinegar. Wine is made when the yeast consumes the sugar and produces alcohol. Vinegar is another fermentation that takes place when we introduce "mother of vinegar," or acetobacters, to wine that has been diluted to about 7% alcohol. Our homemade wines are about 11–11½% alcohol, as are most commercial wines. The acetobacters consume the alcohol and convert it to acetic acid.

There is no mistaking when the conversion takes place. It definitely tastes like vinegar—not like wine at all. Winemaking suppliers sell red and white wine vinegar cultures. Some sell cider, malt and mead cultures as well. It is important to sanitize all utensils and containers that will touch the vinegar by soaking them for 20 minutes in a solution of 30 mL (2 tbsp) chlorine laundry bleach to 4 L (1 gal) water. Rinse everything well with hot tap water.

VINEGAR Method Directions

Into a sanitized glass, enamel, stainless steel or stoneware container, pour:

2 measures dry wine, 11–12% alcohol (I have used Saskatoon Wine and Raspberry Wine successfully.)

1 measure water (boiled 15 minutes and allowed to cool)

1 measure vinegar culture with active bacteria

Cover the container with cheesecloth tied with a string or elastic to keep insects out while allowing air to freely reach mixture. Store in a warm, dark place, 25–30°C (77–86°F). It will take 6 or 8 weeks to convert to vinegar.

An acetic film called "mother" will form. This smooth, leathery, grayish film becomes quite thick and heavy. It should not be disturbed. It often becomes heavy enough to fall and is succeeded by another formation. If the mother falls, remove and discard it. An acid test will indicate when all of the alcohol is converted to vinegar. Part of the vinegar may be withdrawn and pasteurized. The remaining unpasteurized vinegar may be used as a culture to start another batch. Living bacteria are in the liquid. A piece of the mother is not necessary to start a new batch.

Your vinegar may be preserved by pasteurizing, which kills the bacteria. Heat the vinegar to 32°C (90°F) and hold the temperature for 30 minutes. Pasteurized vinegar keeps indefinitely when tightly capped and stored in a dark place at room temperature.

Making vinegar is a bit of a tricky business, but rewarding in a pioneering kind of way!

WILD FRUITS
Recipes from the Garden & from the Wild

LOUISE PATTERSON BRUNS

Harvesting Wild Berries

Harvesting our native wild fruits has been a passion of mine since I was a small child. In the early '50s I remember Mom and Grandma packing a lunch and loading us all in the old green Chev truck and heading up to the berry patches on our farm. Each of us kids would have a tin can punched with a hole in the top and tied onto our belt loops with binder twine. Mom and Grandma went armed with 2½–gallon milk pails. They were serious pickers, because this was their winter fruit supply for the sweet treats they would whip up for our family.

Wild raspberries, gooseberries, black currants, Saskatoons, chokecherries and strawberries all grow in our area even today for those intrepid enough to know their secret hiding places and go after them. Spending an afternoon on a warm hillside picking Saskatoons, crashing through woods searching for wild gooseberries, or wading knee deep in the creek after wild black currants has its delicious rewards in the jams, jellies and wines we make today.

Juicing Wild Fruits

We used to always add a little water and boil the wild fruit, then pour it into a cotton bag and hang it on a kitchen doorknob to drip into a bowl, giving it a good squeeze after it cooled. Then we would go around for a couple of days with purple hands, not to mention splashes of juice on the counter. Nowadays my favourite tool at berry time is my Steam Juicer, a three–layered contraption that holds the fruit in the top sieve, over the collecting pan, with hose attached, which sits on the bottom pan that is full of water. We never have to touch the fruit after it goes in the juicer, and the juice comes out hot and clear as a bell, ready for making jelly, syrup or wine.

BLACK Currant & Saskatoon Jelly

This combination is actually a compliment to both fruits. The black currants are not too strong, and the Saskatoon flavour comes through!

1 pkg	pectin crystals—Certo, Co-op or other
625 mL (2½ c)	black currant juice
625 mL (2½ c)	Saskatoon juice
1¾ kg (6½ c)	sugar

Stir pectin crystals into juice and bring to a boil for 1 minute. Stir in sugar all at once, bring to hard rolling boil for 2 minutes. If it is not jelling at this point, add another 125 mL (½ c) sugar and boil 1 more minute. Pour into 125 mL or 250 mL (½ c or 1 c) sterilized jars and seal.

Wild Gooseberry Jam is so precious that we save it for special occasions, or give a few jars for Christmas to those who really love it.

It is so rare to get enough Wild Strawberries to make jam, that it is a once-in-a-decade specialty.

Other Wild Fruit

Wild cranberries, blueberries, huckleberries and pin cherries can also be found if you are willing to drive to the mountains or a little farther afield in the Chinook Zone. We are willing to go anywhere from Rocky Mountain House to Pincher Creek in search of exotic wild berries!

HELPFUL HINTS

Wild gooseberries when picked green are wildlife free. Also, soak gooseberries, saskatoons or currants in cold water and discard floaters.

DOMESTIC Fruits

LOUISE PATTERSON BRUNS

MANY GARDENERS NOW HAVE AN ABUNDANT SUPPLY OF DOMESTIC fruits. We are cultivating red, black and white currants, raspberries, Saskatoons, chokecherries, Nanking Cherries, Dolgo, Rescue Crabapples, Heyer #12, Patterson and Parkland Apples. There are many more cultivars available for the Prairies. But we make good use of crabapple juice for jellies and wine and, especially, for a delicious breakfast juice. It keeps best in the freezer, though we do can it in jars to be used within 3 months.

The Heyer #12 Apples are our favourites for making a chunky applesauce for pies and apple crisps.

We always serve red or white currant jelly with chicken, turkey, veal or wild game.

There is such an abundance of rhubarb in our garden that we fill the trunk of the car to give away. We also make juice, jelly, jam and wines with rhubarb, sometimes in combination with other fruits.

Recently we have begun to make quantities of canned mixed fruit—Saskatoons, raspberries and rhubarb to use through the winter, served with ice cream, with cereal in the morning, or at the bottom of an upside down cake.

I have been making wine since 1998, and am now on my 100th batch! Most of the wines are from our wild and domestic fruits, though I did start out with wine kits from the store. The homemade wines range from so-so to excellent, but they take a lot of patience. Some of my wines sit for 2 years in the big carboy before they are ready to bottle. I just brought up some 5-year-old Saskatoon wine, and it was a rich, mellow burgundy. Some of the sherry-type sweeter wines are great after a year or two.

HOME Canning of Fruits & Vegetables

LOUISE PATTERSON BRUNS

I COME FROM A LONG LINE OF CANNERS AND PRESERVERS, AND I CAN say that a day or two spent in the kitchen preserving summer's bounty is one of homemaking's peculiar joys. My friends think I am a fanatic, but they sure enjoy those jars of pickles, jellies and chutneys at Christmas!

I would like to stress the importance of canning fruits and vegetables in the safest manner possible. I have even canned meats, always with a pressure canner and following strict procedures outlined by the manufacturer.

Acid Fruits

The easiest foods to can are the acid fruits, as they require only a boiling-water bath in a basic canning kettle. Peaches, pears, applesauce, plums, apricots and cherries are easy to do.

Basic boiling-water bath method:
1. Wash jars and lids in hot soapy water and rinse with boiling water.
2. Prepare syrup.
   Light syrup: 250 mL (1c) sugar to 500 mL (2 c) water
   Medium syrup: 375 mL (1½ c) sugar to 500 mL (2 c) water
   Heavy syrup: 250 mL (1c) sugar to 500 mL (2 c) water
   Mix together in stainless steel pot and bring to a boil.
3. Clean fruit and remove stones if necessary. Pack into jars.
4. Pour syrup over fruit to within ½ cm (¼ in) of rim. Run your finger over the rim to remove any fruit bits and to check for chips in the rim. If there is a chip, throw out the jar. It will not seal.
5. Put on the tin lid—it must be wet to form a good seal—and screw on the ring fairly tight.
6. Put jars in canner and fill with water 2½ cm (1 in) over the top of the tallest jar. Put on the lid and put over high heat. Bring to a rolling boil. Timing starts when the boiling starts! Remember that you are cooking the fruit as well as bringing it to a temperature at which the jar will seal. Use a recipe. Most fruits require 20 to 25 minutes.

7. Remove the jars with a special jar lifter and place them onto a towel on the counter, being careful not to let them touch. Do not touch the lids while cooling. A strong vacuum seal will occur, which you will hear as a satisfying "click" as each jar seals.
8. When the jars are cool and sealed, preferably the next day, be sure to wash them in soapy water, as sometimes they are sticky from the canning procedure.
9. Label and store in a cool dark place. Enjoy!

   Pickles, jams and jellies have high enough acid or sugar contents to be safely canned and sealed in the boiling-water bath.

Non-acid Vegetables, Meats and Fish

If you want to can non-acid vegetables or mixtures, you must use a pressure canner. This is essential to kill the highly toxic botulism, which only the high temperatures of a pressure canner can do. Beans, peas, carrots, onions, garlic, and mixtures containing them, can be deadly if not properly processed.

BLACK CURRANT Syrup

PATTY WEBB

1½ L (6 c)	black currants
250 mL (1 c)	white sugar
250 mL (1 c)	water
75 mL (⅓ c)	corn syrup
10 mL (2 tsp)	lemon juice

Combine all ingredients in a large pot. Heat and stir until it boils. Simmer covered for 10 minutes. Strain. Pour hot syrup into jars. Seal. Very tasty on French toast and cream cheese.

Makes 500 mL (2 half-pints).

Farmers' markets also offer artisans a chance to display their wares. Here we see Franco LoPinto and his wonderful blue pottery at the Millarville Farmers Market.

CHOKECHERRY Jelly

Chokecherries contain little or no pectin, so in order to make them jell, the use of pectin-rich crabapples or pectin is essential. If jelly does not jell, it still makes delicious pancake syrup or base for a cool summer drink.

1 L (4 c)	chokecherry juice
1 L (4 c)	crabapple juice
2 kg (8 c)	sugar
1	bottle pectin

To prepare juice: Wash and clean about a 4-L (1-gal) pail of berries. Add 1 L (4 c) water and boil until tender. Put in jelly bag and drain juice off. Do the same with crabapples.

Measure 500 mL (2 c) each of chokecherry juice and crabapple juice into large, heavy saucepan. Bring to boil and add 1 kg (4 c) sugar, stirring to dissolve sugar. Bring to full rolling boil and add ½ bottle pectin. Boil hard for 1 minute. Test for jelling. Using a shiny spoon, dip in the jelly and let it run off spoon. When drops thicken along edge of spoon and run together before falling off, jelly is ready. Remove from heat. Stir and skim. Pour into hot, sterilized jelly glasses and cover with wax immediately. Repeat with other batch. It is best not to try making too big a batch at one time. Smaller quantities seem to jell best.

CHOKECHERRY Syrup

2¼ kg (8½ c)   chokecherries

625 mL (2½ c)   water

2¼ kg (8½ c)   sugar

Boil, covered, for 15 minutes. Place in jelly bag, squeeze out juice. Yields 1 L (4 c) juice. Put juice in a large pan and add the sugar. Boil for 1 minute. Pour in sterilized jars and seal. Very good on pancakes.

Wild CRANBERRY Jelly

ANNE VALE

The taste of this jelly always reminds me of the silence of the forest where they grow and the picking expeditions with the scent of pine needles, moss and damp soil. The wild low-bush cranberry grows in abundance in our pine forests. Pick in fall after a few frosts have sweetened them. They look very much like kinnikinick but are shinier, and berries are smaller with a distinct blueberry-like dimple at the bottom, and a brighter crimson colour.

1 kg (4 c)   wild cranberries

30 mL (2 tbsp)   lemon juice

1¾ kg (7 c)   sugar

250 mL (1 c)   water

1 packet   fruit pectin

Wash the berries. Using a large saucepan simmer all ingredients except pectin. Bring to a full rolling boil and boil hard for one minute, stirring constantly. Stir in pectin. Stir and skim off foam for a few minutes. Use small canning jars and seal with wax. Wonderful with poultry dishes.

GOOSEBERRY Jam

MARLENE LAMONTAGNE

500 mL (2 c)	gooseberries
500 mL (2 c)	water
180 mL (¾ c)	white sugar to each 250 mL (1 c) cooked fruit

Cook berries in water until soft, then mash and measure the cooked fruit. Add sugar, stir well, and boil rapidly to jellying point (when jam forms slow drop off the edge of spoon).

SASKATOON Jelly

1.875 kg (7½ c)	sugar
750 mL (3 c)	berry juice
125 mL (½ c)	lemon juice (4 lemons), strained
1 bottle	liquid pectin

To prepare fruit: clean ripened berries (about 2 kg/4 lb). Place in kettle and crush. Heat gently until juice starts to flow, then simmer covered 15 minutes. Place in jelly cloth and squeeze out juice.

To make jelly: Measure sugar and juice into large saucepan and mix. Add lemon juice and combine well. Bring to boil over high heat and add all the pectin at once, stirring constantly. Then bring to full rolling boil and boil hard for 1 minute. Remove from heat, skim, pour quickly into jars and seal with wax.

SASKATOON & Rhubarb Jam

1 L (1 qt)	rhubarb
1 L (1 qt)	Saskatoons
750 g (3 c)	sugar

Cut rhubarb in small pieces and put in covered saucepan with Saskatoons and a little water. Bring mixture to boil. Cook until desired thickness. Add sugar and bring to boil. Pour into jars and seal.

BEET Jelly

IDA WEGELIN

The grape Kool Aid allows this jelly to pass as grape jelly.

4	large beets
1½ L (6 c)	beet juice
2–3 oz packages	lemon Jello
2 boxes	Certo
2¼ kg (9 c)	sugar
1 pkg	grape Kool Aid (optional)

Cover peeled and cut-up beets with enough water to make 1½ L (6 c) juice. Measure juice and add Jello, Certo and Kool Aid. Bring to boil then add sugar. Boil for 1 minute, stirring constantly. Skim and pour into jars. Seal while hot.

Yield: 5½–473 mL (16 oz) jars.

This team of Percherons at the Bar U Ranch National Historic
Site brings back memories of the good old days.

Carrot MARMALADE

IDA WEGELIN

5	oranges
3	lemons
12	medium-sized carrots
	sugar
1 tin	crushed pineapple
(473 mL/16 oz)	

Peel oranges and lemons. Cover peel with cold water and let stand overnight. Drain off water and put peel through chopper. Peel and dice carrots or put them through a chopper. Cook orange peel, lemon peel and carrots in as little water as possible. Measure mixture—for every 250 mL (1 c) of mixture add 150 mL (⅔ c) sugar. Add pineapple and finely chopped fruit pulp. Boil mixture until fruit is clear and mixture is thick. Sometimes we add a drained 177-mL (6-oz) jar of maraschino cherries just before putting marmalade into jars—they add colour. Pour into sterilized jars and seal.

CRABAPPLE Jelly

Cover apples with water just until they float. Boil 20 minutes or until they are cooked down. Put in cheesecloth to drip overnight. Measure out 2½ L (10 c) of juice and 2½ kg (10 c) sugar. Put in large kettle and bring to boil. Boil until it foams up once (about 25 minutes). Skim off foam and pour into clean jars. Seal with wax.

Crabapple & ROWAN JELLY

Use an equal weight of crab apples and Rowans (Mountain Ash berries). Cut crab apples into pieces and Rowans off the stem. Put in kettle with enough water, just showing through the fruit. Boil till soft. Pour into jelly bag. When strained, add cup for cup of granulated sugar. Boil till jellying stage. Test frequently as Rowans are rich in pectin. Pour into sterilized jars and seal.

GREEN TOMATO Mincemeat

3 L (3 qt)	finely chopped green tomatoes

Cover with water and boil 1 hour. Let stand overnight and drain.

	salt
1 L (1 qt)	finely chopped apples
1¼ kg (2½ lb)	brown sugar
250 g (½ lb)	mixed peel
500 g (1 lb)	raisins
250 g (½ lb)	currants
250 g (½ lb)	suet
250 mL (1 c)	vinegar
5 mL (1 tsp)	cinnamon
5 mL (1 tsp)	cloves
5 mL (1 tsp)	nutmeg

Mix above ingredients with tomatoes. Bring to a boil for 5 minutes. Bottle and seal hot.

MINT Jelly

250 mL (1 c)	fresh mint leaves
50 mL (¼ c)	boiling water
680 mL (2¾ c)	sugar
1 L (1 qt)	crabapple juice

Wash mint leaves, snip from stems, add boiling water and 625 mL (2½ c) of the sugar. Let stand a few hours. Bring to boiling point, strain through several layers of cheesecloth. Add remaining 50 mL (¼ c) sugar to apple juice, stir until it reacts to jelly test. Skim and pour into hot sterilized jelly glasses. Seal with paraffin.

NANKING Cherry Jelly

PATTY WEBB

    4 L (4 qt)   cherries

Simmer with no water until fruit is soft and mushy. Extract juice.

    1 box   Certo crystals

    1½ L (6 c)   prepared juice

    1¾ L (7 c)   sugar

Mix Certo crystals with prepared juice in large saucepan. On high heat bring to a full boil, stirring. Stir in sugar. Cook and stir until it comes to a rolling boil. Boil hard 1 minute, stirring constantly. Remove from heat and skim if necessary. Pour into sterilized jars and seal.

Makes 2¼ L (9 c).

QUICK Raspberry Jam

Use a fairly large, heavy pan. To each heaping 250 mL (1 c) of raspberries, allow 180 mL (¾ c) sugar. Put fruit and half of sugar in pan. Bring to boil, being careful not to let it stick. Add remaining sugar. Bring to full rolling boil and time 1½ minutes, stirring gently. Take off fire and put in sterilized jars. This method retains fresh fruit colour and flavour.

RHUBARB & Fig Jam

Cut any amount of rhubarb into small pieces, mix with half the amount of sugar and let stand 12–15 hours. Boil till thick. Add cooked figs cut in small pieces and return to boil. Pour into jars and seal.

Rhubarb CONSERVE

3½ kg (14 c)	rhubarb
750 g (3 c)	raisins
1¾ kg (7 c)	sugar
2	oranges, juice of
2	oranges, rind of, thinly sliced
125–250 mL (½–1 c)	chopped walnuts

Combine first 5 ingredients and let stand ½ hour. Bring to boil and boil uncovered for 40 minutes, stirring frequently. Add chopped walnuts and boil to jam stage, about 5 minutes. Pour into hot, sterilized jars. Cool and seal.

Yields 3 L (12 c).

Rhubarb JELLO JAM

DODE ANDERSON

2¼ L (5 c) rhubarb

750 mL (3 c) sugar

1 30-mL (3-oz) jelly powder,
package preferably strawberry

Combine fruit and 250 mL (1 c) of the sugar in large bowl and allow to stand overnight. In the morning, transfer to large preserving kettle and add the remaining sugar and cook until soft. When soft add jelly powder. Stir well, pour into hot sterilized jars. Cover with paraffin wax.

This is a very fast recipe and quite delicious. It certainly uses up all of that extra rhubarb you have.

ZUCCHINI Butter

2 kg (4 lb) zucchini or vegetable marrow

Steam until tender. Drain well and add 125 mL (½ lb) butter, 2 kg (4 lb) sugar, 6 lemons (rind and juice). Mash. Simmer 10 minutes or until a smooth paste. Add preserved ginger if you like it that way.

Zucchini MARMALADE

A good way to use up over-sized zucchini. Peel and remove seeds. Chop and measure:

1½ kg (6 c) zucchini

1½ kg (6 c) sugar

1 large orange

1 lemon, zest of

Let stand overnight. Bring to boil. Simmer for 1 hour. Seal in jars.

PICKLED Beets

Cook beets until tender and peel. Cut in desired pieces. Heat enough vinegar to cover beets, using 250 mL (1 c) sugar to 250 mL (1 c) vinegar, and add salt to taste. When vinegar mixture is boiling, add cut-up beets and bring to boiling point again. Put into sterilized jars and seal. If desired, a few whole cloves and allspice may be added to each jar. These may be drained, butter added, heated and served as a vegetable.

Bread & Butter PICKLES

6 L (6 qt)	cucumbers
2	red peppers
125 mL (½ c)	salt
750 mL (3 c)	sugar
15 mL (3 tsp)	turmeric
15 mL (3 tsp)	celery seed
12	medium onions
1½ L (6 c)	vinegar
	whole cloves
30 mL (2 tbsp)	mustard seed

Cook together until cucumbers appear clear. Bottle hot.

DILLED Vegetables

LOUISE PATTERSON BRUNS

We have made dills out of everything from carrots to green and yellow beans, peppers and asparagus. It is interesting to put several varieties in one jar for a winter treat.

Dilled CARROTS

HAROLD FRANCIS

BRINE MIX

500 mL (2 c)	white vinegar
1 L (4 c)	water
125 mL (½ c)	pickling salt

These are the proportions for the basic brine mix. Make as much or as little depending on how many jars of carrots you want.

Bring brine mix to a rolling boil.

Peel carrots absolutely clean and divide into quarters or eighths (depending on diameter). Cut these into pieces about 7–10 cm (3–4 in) long. Pack carrots into jars, keeping in mind that the tighter the pack, the longer the cure time. Add dill weed and 2 to 3 garlic cloves. Pour the boiling brine mix over carrots to fill jars to the top making sure there are no air bubbles. Seal and store for 3 to 4 months.

PICKLED Carrots (Litre/Quart Size)

1 L (1 qt)	small carrots
750 mL (3 c)	white vinegar
125 mL (½ c)	water
250 mL (1 c)	sugar
45 mL (3 tbsp)	pickling spice

Cook carrots until skins slip off easily and carrots are half done. Slip off skins. Boil together 10 minutes the vinegar, water, sugar and spice. Remove spice. Add carrots and boil 2–4 minutes or until tender. Pack in hot, sterile jars, pour syrup over and seal.

Variation: Pickled shoestring carrots for cocktail. Cut carrots after parboiling into uniform strips. Follow the above directions but do not boil the sticks in syrup. Barely bring them to boiling point. Pack and seal.

Canned COLESLAW

2	heads cabbage, shredded fine
6	carrots, shredded fine
2	onions, chopped fine
2	red peppers (sweet)
125 mL (½ c)	salt

Cover with cold water. Let sit 3 hours. Drain well. Pack into jars, leaving 1 cm (½ in) head space.

Boil together:

1 L (1 qt)	white vinegar
1.25 L (5 c)	sugar
5 mL (1 tsp)	celery seed
5 mL (1 tsp)	mustard seed

Pour into jars. Seal.

Spiced CRABAPPLES

Select good-flavoured, rosy-cheeked crabapples. Wash well, leaving stems on. Remove the blossom ends and prick with needle several times. These are delicious served with pork, chicken or ham.

750 mL (3 c)	vinegar
750 mL (3 c)	water or beet water from cooking beets
1½ kg (6 c)	sugar (or less)
5 mL (1 tsp)	whole cloves
1 8-cm (3-in)	stick cinnamon
3 kg (6 lb)	crabapples

Put vinegar, water, sugar and spices (tied in bag) in kettle and boil for 5 minutes. Add crabapples and simmer gently till tender, but do not overcook. Pack in sterilized jars, cover with boiling syrup and seal.

Another method: Pack raw apples into hot jars, cover with boiling syrup and process in hot water bath for 20 minutes.

EVERLASTING Salad

1	cabbage
5	carrots
4	onions
4	peppers
50 mL (¼ c)	salt
5 mL (1 tsp)	celery seed
5 mL (1 tsp)	mustard seed
500 mL (2 c)	sugar
500 mL (2 c)	vinegar (white)

Shred vegetables, add salt and let stand 2 hours. Drain well and add other ingredients. Put in jars and keep refrigerated. This salad can be processed in hot water bath for 20 minutes in sealed jars.

GREEN Tomato Pickles (Sweet)

4 kg (8 lb)	peeled tomatoes

Sprinkle with 125 mL (½ c) salt and let stand overnight. Drain.

1½ kg (6 c)	sugar
1 L (1 qt)	vinegar
15 mL (½ oz)	whole cloves
6	sticks cinnamon

Boil tomatoes in this until tender. Let stand 2 days. Drain. Boil juice and pour over tomatoes. Repeat twice from "let stand." Put tomatoes in jars. Boil juice and seal hot.

Greg Perry of Whiskey Creek Greenhouse offers a mouth-watering taste test.

Green Tomato PICKLES

4½ L (1 gal)	sliced green tomatoes
4	large onions, chopped
4 or 5	stalks celery (chopped)
1	red pepper, chopped
1	green pepper, chopped

Put vegetables in crock and cover with 180 mL (¾ c) pickling salt. Cover with boiling water and leave overnight. Drain well. (If tomatoes are very green, wash in cold water and drain again.) To vegetables, add:

500 mL (2 c)	vinegar
875–1000 mL (3½–4 c)	sugar
15 mL (1 tbsp)	celery seed
15 mL (1 tbsp)	mustard seed
5 mL (1 tsp)	turmeric
125 mL (½ c)	pickling spice in cotton bag (only 15 minutes)
500 mL (2 c)	apple sauce (or crabapple butter)

Simmer for 1 hour and bottle in clean, sterilized jars.

THOUSAND ISLE Pickle

8	cucumbers
12	large onions
1	large cauliflower
2	red peppers
2	green peppers
125 mL (½ c)	salt
1¼ L (5 c)	water

SAUCE

2 L (8 c)	mild vinegar
1½ kg (6 c)	sugar
15 mL (1 tbsp)	mustard seed
15 mL (1 tbsp)	celery seed
180 mL (¾ c)	flour
15 mL (1 tbsp)	dry mustard
15 mL (1 tbsp)	turmeric

Chop vegetables, soak 1 hour in salt and water and strain. Put vegetables in sauce and boil 20 minutes. Bottle.

Zucchini PICKLES

1 kg (2 lb)	small zucchini
2	medium onions
50 mL (¼ c)	salt
500 mL (1 pt)	white vinegar
250 mL (1 c)	sugar
5 mL (1 tsp)	celery seed
5 mL (1 tsp)	mustard seed
5 mL (1 tsp)	turmeric
2 mL (½ tsp)	dry mustard

Wash and cut unpeeled zucchini and peeled onions in very thin slices into crock or bowl. Cover with water, add salt. Let stand 1 hour. Drain. Mix remaining ingredients and bring to boil. Pour over zucchini-onion mixture. Let stand 1 hour. Bring to boil and cook 3 minutes. Pack in hot, sterilized jars to within 1 cm (½ in) of top and seal.

Yields 1½ L (3 pt).

Zucchini BREAD & Butter Pickles

DODE ANDERSON

This is a wonderful recipe to use up the mountains of zucchini a few plants produce. Don't leave your car unlocked during zucchini season as your friends will undoubtedly find a place to get rid of their extras.

4 L (4 qt)	sliced zucchini (approx. 8 zucchini)
6	sliced white onions
2	green peppers, chopped
2	red peppers, chopped
2	cloves garlic, chopped very fine
125 mL (½ c)	pickling salt
	cracked ice

Put everything in a crock with cracked ice over top. Let stand 3 hours. Drain, but do not wash.

SYRUP

1¼ L (5 c)	sugar
750 mL (3 c)	cider vinegar
7 mL (1½ tsp)	turmeric powder
5 mL (1 tsp)	celery seed

Bring syrup ingredients to boil and add drained vegetables. Boil about 20 minutes. Pack into sterilized jars.

CHILI Sauce

1.875 kg (7½ lb)   ripe tomatoes, peeled and chopped

Grind in food chopper:

6   medium onions
(625 g/2½ c)

6   red and green peppers, mixed
(625 g/2½ c)

750 mL (3 c)   celery, finely shredded or chopped

Put in large kettle and add:

750 mL (3 c)   sugar

30 mL (2 tbsp)   salt

1 L (4 c)   cider vinegar

1½   sticks cinnamon

15 mL (1 tbsp)   garlic salt

In cheesecloth bag put:

15 mL (1 tbsp)   whole cloves

45 mL (3 tbsp)   whole allspice

Drop the bag in mixture and cook for 2½–3 hours. This sauce has a superb flavour. Put in hot jars and seal.

Makes about 4 L (8 pt).

MINT Sauce

Prepare 1 L (4 c) of ground mint leaves. Use only the leaves, not the stems. Wash and dry mint leaves. Put through fine screen on food chopper. Boil 500 mL (2 c) sugar in 1 L (1 qt) vinegar for 1 minute. Add mint leaves and simmer for 10 minutes. Pour into jars and seal. Goes well with lamb.

Tomato SALSA

THERESA PATTERSON

When you have masses of ripe tomatoes in the fall try this one. The tomatoes can be any size, from small cherry ones on up, it doesn't matter—just chop up the bigger ones. You don't need to peel them either.

In a large saucepan or Dutch oven put in a quantity of washed and cut-up tomatoes. Then add 4 or 5 chopped onions, 4 chopped red peppers, 4 or 5 cloves garlic, chopped. Place on medium heat and bring to a boil. Seasonings are optional—try a few chili flakes or more if you like it hot, some garlic powder, salt and pepper, and some brown sugar. Then add 50–75 mL (¼–⅓ c) of balsamic vinegar.

Cover and bake in oven until well done (1 hour or more) and somewhat reduced in quantity. Adjust seasonings to suit your taste. Cool and put in plastic containers in freezer.

This has a lovely fresh taste. Use with meats, chicken, eggs or on crackers.

Autumn Medley BRUSCHETTA

LOUISE PATTERSON BRUNS

eggplant

olive oil

balsamic vinegar

wine

spices

salt

onion

roasted tomatoes

garlic

sweet peppers

Before combining ingredients, sprinkle eggplant with salt and drain for a couple of hours (this reduces bitterness).

In a roasting pan or baking dish, combine 2 tbsp. olive oil, 1 tbsp. balsamic vinegar, 2 tbsp. wine, some Italian seasoning, oregano and your favourite herb blend, such as Garlic Plus or Garlic and Red Peppers. Add salt to taste.

Add chopped onions, tomatoes, garlic, sweet peppers and eggplant, stirring them into the oil and herb mixture. Add more oil and herb mixture if needed.

Bake at 180°C (350°F) for 30 minutes, then scrape the edges of the baking dish as the juice begins to reduce. Continue baking until the bruschetta is the consistency you like.

This recipe will fill your kitchen with a wonderful aroma.

Serving suggestions:
Great with cheese and crackers and a bottle of wine.

Spread on a baguette split lengthwise, top with cheese, and toast under the broiler.

Braided Onions

Beet RELISH

IDA WEGELIN

2 kg (4 lb)	beets (18 medium)
4	medium onions
½ kg (1 lb)	sweet red peppers

Wash and peel raw beets and onions, and wash and remove the seeds from peppers. Grind all vegetables raw through a coarse chopper. Heat to boiling the following sauce:

750 mL (3 c)	vinegar
10 mL (2 tsp)	salt
500 mL (2 c)	sugar

Tie 30 mL (2 tbsp) mixed pickling spices in a piece of cheesecloth and place along with vegetables into the hot sauce. Let simmer (uncovered) for 30 minutes. Remove spice bag and bottle, making sure the relish is covered with juice. Seal. Horseradish may be added if desired.

HAMBURGER Relish

12	large ripe tomatoes
12	large apples, chopped
9	medium onions, chopped
500 mL (2 c)	sugar
500 mL (1 pt)	white vinegar
5 mL (1 tsp)	pepper
2 mL (½ tsp)	celery salt
2 mL (½ tsp)	cloves
2 mL (½ tsp)	allspice
5 mL (1 tsp)	cinnamon
50 mL (¼ c)	salt

Blend all ingredients. Cook until thick. Pour while hot into sterilized jars. Seal.

GRANDMA'S Corn Relish

PATTY WEBB

This is my husband's Grandmother's recipe. She grew an outstanding vegetable garden in a vacant lot in Medicine Hat. The conditions for growing corn were superior to our frosty area where we have to take extra care and precautions to get our corn to the mature state.

1 L (4 c)	fresh corn (9 cobs) or frozen corn
1	green pepper, seeded and finely chopped
1	red pepper, seeded and finely chopped
1	medium onion, finely chopped
125 mL (½ c)	finely chopped celery
2 mL (½ tsp)	salt
550 mL (2¼ c)	white sugar
550 mL (2¼ c)	white vinegar
2 mL (½ tsp)	celery seed
2 mL (½ tsp)	dry mustard powder
15 mL (1 tbsp)	cornstarch
2 mL (½ tsp)	turmeric
30 mL (2 tbsp)	water

Place the corn in a large pot. Add green and red peppers, onion, celery, salt, sugar, vinegar and celery seed. Stir and bring to a boil, turn heat down and simmer for about 30 minutes and continue to stir. Mix mustard powder, cornstarch, turmeric and water in a small bowl and add to simmering corn mixture. Stir until it thickens. Pour into jars and seal.

Makes 1½ L (6 half-pints).

HORSERADISH

Dig roots in late fall or early spring (months with "R" in them). Peel under water. Cut in short lengths. Grind (outside in open air). Add 500 mL (2 c) white sugar and enough white vinegar to cover; enough for 4 L (1 gal) of ground horseradish mix. Place in sterilized jars, leaving head room, and freeze. To serve, add more vinegar and sugar if it seems dry. Great with roast beef. In hard times, use with cottage cheese.

RHUBARB Relish

IDA WEGELIN

1 L (4 c)	rhubarb
500 mL (2 c)	onions
500 mL (2 c)	vinegar
500 mL (2 c)	brown sugar
5 mL (1 tsp)	salt
5 mL (1 tsp)	cloves
5 mL (1 tsp)	ginger
5 mL (1 tsp)	cinnamon
5 mL (1 tsp)	allspice

Combine ingredients. Boil until thick. Bottle and seal. Good with steak and beef roasts. (If desired, raisins may be added.)

SAUERKRAUT

DOROTHY JACKSON

EXTRA CABBAGE CAN EASILY BE MADE INTO THIS OLD-FASHIONED vegetable. If you feel like experimenting with a small batch, a 4-L (1-gal) jar will hold slightly over 2½ kg (5 lb) of cabbage or an 8-L (2-gal) crock holds 7½ kg (15 lb) cabbage. Choose sound, mature cabbage, use ½ kg (1 lb) salt for 20 kg (40 lb) of cabbage or 10 mL (2 tsp) salt for ½ kg (1 lb) cabbage. European flavour can be added with use of dill, a bay leaf, a few garlic cloves (peeled but whole so that they can be fished out before serving), or onion rings or some favourite whole pickling spice.

Never mix a fresh batch of sauerkraut with one already fermenting. A top-quality vegetable should release enough juice to form a covering brine in about 24 hours. If it hasn't, bring level above shredded cabbage by adding a weak brine, proportions of 7 mL (1½ tsp) of pickling salt for each 250 mL (1 c) of cold water.

Remove outside leaves, quarter heads and cut out cores. Slice cabbage fine into 15-cm (6-in) shreds and mix with pickling salt. Pack containers with alternate layers of salt and cabbage, as in amount indicated above. Tamp every 2 layers of cabbage to get rid of trapped air and start the juice flow. Tap gently with clean wooden potato masher or bottom of small jar or clean baseball bat. Pack firmly in jars or crocks to within 5 cm (2 in) of top. Cover with clean cloth and a plate or any board except pine. Place weight on plate, heavy enough to make the brine come up to the cover and wet the cloth. When fermentation begins, remove scum daily and replace clean cloth over the cabbage. Wash plate daily also.

Best quality kraut results when made at a temperature below 15°C (60°F), requiring at least a month of fermentation. It may be cured in less time at higher temperature, but the kraut will not be as good. If sauerkraut turns tan, too much juice has been lost in the fermenting process. When fermenting ceases, store kraut in cool place. If it is not around 3°C (38°F) you had better process it. For the canning process, heat kraut to simmering temperature (about 82°C/180°F), pack firmly into hot jars; add sufficient kraut juice or weak brine (30 mL/2 tbsp salt to 1 L/1 qt water) to cover, leaving 1 cm (½ in) head space. Process in a boiling-water bath, 25 minutes, for pints 30 minutes. Cook kraut 15 minutes before serving.

RIPE TOMATO Chutney

14	medium-sized ripe tomatoes, peeled
7	apples, peeled and cut in pieces
7	medium onions, chopped
500 mL (2 c)	vinegar
375 mL (¾ lb)	brown sugar
180 mL (¾ c)	white sugar
250 mL (½ lb)	raisins
3 mL (¾ tsp) each	cloves, allspice, ginger and cinnamon
15 mL (1 tbsp)	salt (may need a little more)

Boil all together until thick. Pour into sterilized jars and seal.

Makes about 3½ L (7 pt).

ZUCCHINI Relish

Good way to use up over-sized zucchini.

Peel and grind

    2½ kg (10 c)   zucchini

Grind

    250 mL (1 c)   onion

Add

    75 mL (5 tbsp)   salt

Mix together and let stand overnight. In morning, drain and rinse with cold water. Add:

    550 mL (2¼ c)   vinegar

    1–1½ kg (4–6 c)   sugar

    5 mL (1 tsp)   celery seed

    5 mL (1 tsp)   mustard seed

    2 mL (½ tsp)   pepper

    1   chopped red pepper (large)

Mix all and cook 30 minutes, longer if too watery. Seal.

Makes 4 L (8 pt).

HELPFUL HINT

Put a piece of horseradish in dill pickles for added zip and flavour.

TOASTED Sunflower Seeds

DOROTHY JACKSON

Cut heads off sunflowers when seeds start to turn brown. Hang heads upside down in warm place to dry. Remove seeds and soak overnight in salt water. Dry and then roast in 90°C (200°F) oven for 3 hours or until crisp. Sunflower seeds are very nutritious.

TOASTED Pumpkin Seeds

DOROTHY JACKSON

Method 1
Don't throw away those wet, string-laden seeds from your pumpkin. They are a delicious treat! Wash seeds and remove strings to the best of your ability. Let seeds soak in salted water overnight. (2 mL/½ tsp salt per 150 mL/⅔ c water). Then place seeds in low baking pan in oven at 150°C (300°F) for approximately 20 minutes or till golden. Eat with or without removing shells. Any squash seeds can be prepared in same way, but they are not as tasty as pumpkin.

Method 2
Spread pumpkin seeds over baking sheet. Bake in 190°C (375°F) oven for 30 minutes until seeds dry and fluff up slightly. Stir frequently. Cool. Store in airtight container. Before eating, sprinkle with salt, if desired.

Method 3
Wash fresh pumpkin seeds in a bowl using warm water to remove fibres. Drain and blot dry. Coat seeds with melted butter and spread them out on cookie sheet. Sprinkle seeds to taste with salt. Place in slow oven 120°C (250°F) for 20–30 minutes until they are light golden in colour.

BABY Food

Purée cooked vegetables in a blender using a cooling liquid to bring to a very smooth consistency. Do not add salt, sugar or butter. Carrots, peas, wax beans, green beans and yellow squash are recommended vegetables for babies. Place purée in ice cube containers. *Note:* If you don't have a blender, prepare puréed home-grown vegetables for baby by using a strainer, a sieve or grinder, and freeze. When frozen, empty cubes into a freezer bag, label, date and use as needed. To serve, place frozen or thawed cube in a cup, place in a saucepan with 1 cm (½ in) water and heat.

Washed berries, such as blueberries or Saskatoons, may be pressed through a strainer or food mill to remove the skins and seeds, then frozen in ice cube trays. One litre (one quart) of berries yields approximately 500 mL (2 c) purée or 10 food cubes. Do not add sweetening. Berries such as raspberries and strawberries contain a great many seeds—if you cannot remove the seeds then avoid using these berries. Do not use cranberries.

For more information on preparing baby foods from your home-grown fruits and vegetables, contact your local health clinic.

Start your gardeners while they're young.

FLOWERS as Food

PAM VIPOND

*"Life is too short not to take pleasure
in every bite of every meal;
flowers in, on, and with food
enhance that pleasure, and
help create tables—and moments—
everyone remembers."*

FROM THE EXQUISITE BOOK *ON FLOWERS*
BY KATHRYN KLEINMAN AND SARA SLAVIN

THE FLOWER GARDEN HAS BEEN THE COOK'S EXTENDED KITCHEN garden for generations. Roses were a sacred culinary delight in Pakistan and Morocco for centuries. In the England of King Charles II, court chefs pounded violets and chicory together to make a confection called violet plates. For many Chinese, chrysanthemum petals floating in their soup symbolized future joy. Violets have been crystallized since the days of the ancient Egyptians. Carnation petals are one of the secret ingredients in Chartreuse, a liqueur developed by monks in France in the seventeenth century. England's Queen Elizabeth I is said to have been quite fond of Lavender Tea. In Mexico, "jamaico," a cool infusion made from hibiscus flowers, is the drink of choice on a hot summer's day. Other flower beverages include jasmine tea in Asia and mint tea with orange blossoms floating on top in North Africa.

In North America today, our dependence on supermarkets to provide our food has essentially eliminated flowers from our diets. However, with the upsurge of interest in gardening, good food and good health, flowers have begun to return to our plates. Many people consider a flower on their plate to be decoration only and set it aside but a growing number are including flowers in everyday meals and featuring them in special dishes. Most of us know our favourite herbs and easily add them to many of our

Salad garnished with edible flowers.

family dishes. So it is with flowers. Ten years ago only the most exclusive restaurants included flowers on their menus. Now we are learning to enjoy flowers in many dishes in our own homes. Rose petal ice cream, lavender martinis, and nasturtiums in salads are a wonderful beginning to a new world of taste for all of us to explore.

Which flowers are edible? There are many books that list edible flowers.

The Rules of Eating Edible Flowers
(Adapted from *Edible Flowers* by Cathy Barash)
1. Eat flowers only when you are positive they are edible. Not all flowers are edible. Some are poisonous.
2. Eat only flowers that have been grown organically.
3. Do not eat flowers from florists, nurseries or garden centres.
4. If you have hay fever, asthma or allergies, do not eat fresh flowers.

5. Do not eat flowers picked from the side of the road. They may be contaminated from car emissions or herbicide sprays.
6. There are many varieties of any one flower. Flowers taste different and have different colours when grown in different locations.
7. Introduce flowers into your diet the way you would new foods to a baby—one at a time in small quantities.

The following is a list of common flowers in Southern Alberta that are known to be toxic: bleeding heart, buttercup, clematis, daffodil, datura, delphinium, foxglove, iris, larkspur, lily of the valley, lobelia, lupin, mistletoe, monkshood, morning glory, narcissus, petunia, potato, poinsettia, primrose, sweet pea.

Preparing Flowers for Eating

My suggestion for which part of which flower to eat is simple—if it feels good in your mouth, enjoy it; if not, leave it out of your food. For instance, scented geraniums are edible but the leaves feel like furry lumps in your mouth. Use them as you would bay leaves, cooking them into the dish but removing the leaves before it is served. The petals of daisies, roses, clover and marigolds are wonderful to cook with but the tough centre is unpleasant in the mouth. Pansies and nasturtiums are eaten whole. Separate the individual flowers from the stems for flowers like chives, sage and lilacs. Squash blossoms, tulips, hollyhocks, day lilies and flowers like them require the removal of the stamens and pistils from their centres before they are cooked or stuffed. It is the stamens of the saffron crocus that are dried and become saffron.

Taste the flowers in your garden to get to know their flavours. While a flower may be edible it may not be to your taste. For instance all roses are edible but some taste so metallic that even I will spit them out.

Picking

Pick the flowers when they are just opened. It is best to pick them just before you are going to use them. Be sure they are herbicide-free and pesticide-free.

Washing

Wash flowers as you would fresh herbs—gently in fresh water. If you are concerned about insects, wash them in water with a little salt in it. The salt will remove any insects.

Storage

If the flowers have long enough stems, store them in water in the refrigerator. Otherwise store the blossoms in a plastic bag in the refrigerator. Do not pull the petals off until you are ready to use them. Some flowers, such as pansies, calendula, chives and daisies, will last 4–6 days if they are kept cool; nasturtiums, roses and bergamot will last 2–3 days; tuberous begonias and squash blossoms should be used as soon as possible.

Edible flowers, whether we realize it or not, are already an integral part of our lives. Staple vegetables such as broccoli, cauliflower and artichokes are actually flower buds. Cloves are the dried flower buds of the clove bush.

Use only edible flowers as garnishes.

Flower Petals in Salads

Salads are where most people begin to add flowers to their food. Do taste them first.

All culinary herb flowers are edible. The flowers taste just like the leaves although slightly stronger. Chive blossoms (usually deadheaded and discarded) are fabulous in salads. Always use fresh flowers in salads

Mesclun is a blend of specialty lettuces and herbs often found in produce departments or farmers' markets. The leaves are young and tender. They make a delicious base for a flower petal salad.

Use a delicate dressing so that you do not overpower the flowers' taste. It is best to mix the dressing with the greens and then add the flowers at the last minute.

These flowers are delicious in salads:

Rose petals, pansies, nasturtiums (flowers and leaves), lavender, chive blossoms and all herb flowers, dianthus and pinks, tuberous begonia petals, marigold and calendula petals, borage flowers, daisies petals, tulips and lilacs, scarlet runner bean flowers, bergamot (wild, perennial from your garden or the annual lemon bergamot), sunflower petals, even dandelion petals.

Beyond Salads
Once you have become at ease with eating flowers in salads, a whole new world of dining opens up. The following is an introduction to the possibilities that await you.

Flower BUTTERS

90 mL (6 tbsp)	butter
45 mL (3 tbsp)	chopped flower petals
15 mL (1 tbsp)	lemon juice
	sea salt and fresh ground pepper

Pound the butter with a pestle and mortar until smooth. Add the chopped flower petals gradually, pounding after each addition. (Alternatively use a food processor or blender). Chill until firm.

Any flowers or combination of flowers and herbs can be used for a savory or sweet flavour treat. Try chive blossoms, nasturtiums, lavender, sage, roses (add a little sugar instead of salt), bergamot and pineapple sage.

FLOWER Infusions

Infusions are a fun and endlessly versatile way to add flower flavours and colour to a wide variety of food. Simply add the flowers to the base and let sit for 1–5 days in a cool, dark place or blend the flowers into your base first then let it infuse. Strain out the flower petals if you wish.

Experiment to find your favourites.

Infused oils—basil, nasturtium, marigolds

Infused vinegar—rose petal, lavender, bergamot, nasturtium

Infused wine—clove pinks, rose petals, scented geraniums

Infused vodka for flower martinis—lavender (use a stem of lavender as a garnish), rose, lilac

Infused sugar—rose petals, lavender, clove pinks, scented geraniums

Teas—add fresh petals to your herbal teas

The following is a collection of delicious recipes that include or feature flowers.

Sooke Harbour House
CALENDULA RICE

Sooke Harbour House is an award-winning restaurant on Vancouver Island that has an extensive garden of edible flowers and includes them throughout their menus. Calendula, also called "Poor Man's Saffron," is a mild-flavoured flower that can be added to savoury or sweet dishes.

500 mL (2 c)	chicken broth
300 mL (1¼ c)	fresh calendula petals
1	medium-sized onion, diced
30 mL (2 tbsp)	sunflower seed oil
250 mL (1 c)	brown rice

Blend chicken broth and calendula petals in the blender at high speed until liquified. In a pot, sauté the onion in oil until soft. Add the rice and stir. Make sure all of the grains of rice are coated with oil. At this point, add the calendula liquid and bring the entire mixture to a boil. Then, reduce to low heat. Cover the rice and simmer until all the liquid has been absorbed, which should take from 35–45 minutes. Add the remaining 50 mL (¼ c) of fresh calendula petals as you remove the pot from the heat.

CALENDULA & Orange Cake

CAKE BATTER

5	eggs
125 mL (½ c)	butter, softened to room temperature
375 mL (1½ c)	granulated sugar
2	lemons, grated rind of
1	orange, grated rind of
250 mL (1 c)	sour cream
125 mL (½ c)	plain yogurt
750 mL (3 c)	all-purpose flour
10 mL (2 tsp)	baking soda
125 mL (½ c)	calendula petals, chopped (plus more for garnish)

SYRUP TOPPING

125 mL (½ c)	orange juice
50 mL (¼ c)	Grand Marnier
50 mL (¼ c)	lemon juice
50 mL (¼ c)	granulated sugar

Preheat oven to 180°C (350°F). Separate eggs. Beat whites until they form stiff peaks. Set aside. Cream butter and sugar together. Blend in egg yolks, lemon rind, orange rind, sour cream and yogurt. Beat until smooth. Sift dry ingredients together. Slowly add dry ingredients to wet, mixing well. Gently fold in beaten egg whites and calendula petals.

Butter and flour an angel food cake pan. Pour in cake batter and bake for 60 minutes. Remove from oven and let cool in pan 10 minutes, then remove to a cooling rack and allow to cool completely. Combine all topping ingredients in a saucepan over low heat. Bring to a boil, then simmer for 3 minutes. Pour hot syrup over cooled cake and garnish with calendula petals.

Serves 8 to 12.

An exotic treat from your garden.

ROSES

All varieties of rose are edible. There are variations in flavour, however, so taste before you serve. The stronger the scent, the stronger the flavour.

ROSE Petal Punch

A handful of strongly scented rose petals will delicately flavour a punch for a summer evening. Two or three hours before you want to serve the punch put a good handful of fresh, scented petals into a mixing bowl. Sprinkle a tablespoon of sugar over the roses and pour over it a large bottle of sparkling water and the juice of one lemon. Chill. When ready to serve, strain off the liquid into a punch bowl and add a bottle of red or chilled white wine. Serve in tall glasses.

SCARLET RUNNER BEANS

The runner bean flowers taste like beans with a hint of sweetness and are crunchy in texture. There is a sweet nectar at the base of each flower so don't remove the base. Use to top soups, put in salads, and as a garnish.

HERBED Bean Salad with Scarlet Runner Blossom

¾ kg (1½ lb)	snap beans, topped, tailed and halved
45 mL (3 tbsp)	lemon juice
1	medium shallot, finely minced
50 mL (¼ c)	olive oil
17 mL (1 heaping tbsp)	minced parsley
15 mL (1 tbsp)	minced basil
	salt and pepper
about 125 mL (½ c)	scarlet runner bean blossoms, rinsed and patted dry

Blanch the beans in lightly salted boiling water for 3 or 4 minutes or until tender crisp. Refresh under cold water and drain well. Prepare the vinaigrette while the beans are cooking. In a small bowl, stir the lemon juice, shallot, and olive oil with a fork until blended. Add the herbs, about 1 mL (¼ tsp) salt, and freshly ground pepper to taste. Stir well. Pour the vinaigrette over the warm beans and toss well. Add a little more olive oil if necessary. Cool to room temperature. Toss the blossoms in just before serving.

Pam Vipond, author of our chapter on edible flowers.

Harvesting edible flowers.

SQUASH Blossoms

Use male flowers (those with the single tubular stamen), which don't bare
fruit and so can be harvested in large numbers.

A good flower for stuffing with cheeses, bread crumbs or meat mixtures
and then deep fried. When stuffing, leave the stems on but otherwise remove
the stamens and pistils. The blossoms may be sliced and added to a variety
of dishes including souffles, frittatas, scrambled eggs and burritos.

Note: They wilt quickly so pick just before you are going to use them.

Tuberous BEGONIA

The flowers are crisp in texture and have a spicy, lemony flavour. Add sliced
or chopped petals to sandwiches and salads.

DAY LILIES

Add fresh 2½ cm (1 in) day lily buds to your stir fries.

Scrambled Eggs with CHIVE Flowers

30 mL (2 tbsp)	chive flowers
30 mL (2 tbsp)	chopped chive leaves
15 mL (1 tbsp)	parsley
4	eggs
	salt and pepper
60 mL (4 tbsp)	milk or cream
50 g (1½ oz)	butter

Cut the chive flower head from the stem, then nip off each floret, removing as much of the little stems as possible, 30–40 florets from each head. Chop the chive leaves and parsley very finely and mix with the chive flowers. Beat or whisk the eggs and seasoning together with the milk.

Melt the butter in a heavy-based saucepan. Pour in the egg mixture and cook over a low heat. Stir continuously for a minute or two until the mixture is just beginning to thicken, then add the chive leaves and flowers and the parsley. Serve the scrambled eggs with buttered toast and add a scattering of extra flowers as a garnish.

An assortment of edible flowers.

LAVENDER Lemonade

Lavender is a potent flavour whether fresh or dried. When in doubt, use less.

1¼ L (5 c)	water
125 mL (½ c)	lavender flowers, stripped from stems
75 mL (⅓ c)	freshly squeezed lemon juice
125 mL (½ c)	granulated sugar (more to taste)
	mint leaves for garnish

In a small saucepan on the stove, bring 250 mL (1 c) of the water to a rolling boil. Remove from heat and add lavender flowers. Cover and steep for 20 minutes. Sieve through a fine-meshed sieve, discard the blossoms, and set lavender tea aside. Meanwhile, in a quart jug, mix lemon juice with the remaining water and sugar to taste. Add prepared lavender tea. Serve chilled or hot.

NASTURTIUM Pizza

All parts of the nasturtium are edible. The leaves are delicious in salads and in sand-wiches. The seed pods can be pickled to become "Canadian Capers." The flowers are peppery and make a lovely addition to scrambled eggs, rice dishes, dips and muffins.

For a 25–28 cm (10–11 in) Pizza:

1 pkg	pizza pie crust or your own crust
5 mL (1 tsp)	blended Italian herbs or fresh herbs to your taste
90 mL (3 oz)	Monterey Jack cheese
2 small or 1 large	leek, cleaned, sliced thin, sautéed in olive oil
½	small zucchini, thinly sliced
125 mL (½ c)	asparagus, sliced diagonally
	handful nasturtium flowers
	day lily buds if desired
15 mL (½ oz)	grated parmesan cheese
2 stems	garlic chive blossoms

Prepare pizza crust adding herbs to the dry mixture (or sprinkle on prepared crust). Shape dough into freeform round, 25–28 cm (10–11 in). Bake at 220°C (425°F) on lowest oven rack for 10 minutes. Slice cheese using a cheese plane. Top pizza crust with leeks, zucchini, asparagus, ½ the nasturtiums chopped and the sliced Jack cheese. Bake another 5–7 minutes, until cheese melts. Sprinkle with parmesan and bake a few more minutes until cheese melts. Sprinkle with the rest of the nasturtiums and garlic chive blossoms.

Food DRYING

DOROTHY JACKSON

"WASTE NOT, WANT NOT," IS AS TRUE TODAY AS WHEN THE AXIOM was coined years ago. Drying is the oldest method of food preservation known to man, and is still the most economical. Add to the fun, cut the cost, and increase the variety with food gems you prepare yourself.

You don't have to have a food dryer or take a special course to learn about food drying; these tools help but several dried foods can be prepared at home with only a little basic knowledge and no special equipment. Once you try food drying, however, you'll probably enjoy it so much that you'll want to go further into this old time art!

Dried foods have several advantages:
- they're compact
- they're light weight
- they keep several seasons
- they're healthful: more food value is preserved than by methods using higher heat or water, there are no additives or chemicals
- they taste good
- they're versatile
- they cost little or are even free

What can you dry? Almost anything! Fruits, vegetables, meats, poultry (as jerky), nuts and herbs.

The drying of foods can open up an exciting and interesting new way of preparing food and eating in your home. The possibilities for the use of dried foods are endless. Dry it, you'll like it!

FRUIT Leather

FRUIT LEATHERS ARE FRUIT PURÉES DRIED TO A NON-STICKY, PLIABLE texture. They are sold in health food stores but you can make your own at a fraction of the cost and yours will not contain preservatives. Leathers can be made from single fruits or combinations of two or more, sweetened with honey if you like, made tart with lemon, or flavoured with spices.

Basic Instructions:

1. Use very ripe fruit.
2. Use a blender to reduce fruit to a pulp. Add only enough liquid to blend. (Some fruits blend better if cooked a little first: apples, rhubarb, peaches.)
3. When purée is smooth add desired sweetening. Ripe sweet fruit requires nothing more.
4. Pour a thin layer of purée onto a dehydration tray.
5. Put in dehydrator or on a non-stick cookie sheet in the oven with the setting on low 65–90°C (150–200°F), leaving the oven door open about 2½ cm (1 in).
6. Most leathers will dry in 6 to 12 hours. It depends on the kind of fruit, its thickness and humidity.
7. When leather can be pulled completely free of the tray it is dried. Don't over-dry; it should be chewy but not stiff.
8. Store rolled in plastic wrap or store in tall glass jars.
9. Tear off a piece and start chewing or make into pinwheels.

Fruit Leather PINWHEELS

Spread filling over a sheet of fruit leather. Roll like a cinnamon roll and slice like salami.

125 mL (½ c)	liquid honey
250 mL (1 c)	non-instant dry milk
15 mL (1 tbsp)	butter
2 mL (½ tsp)	vanilla
125–250 mL (½–1 c)	coconut
125 mL (½ c)	chopped nuts (optional—can use peanuts, cashews, sesame seeds)
125 mL (½ c)	ground apples or pears (optional)
1 sheet	fruit leather

Stir, then knead honey, dry milk, butter, vanilla together. Add remaining ingredients and spread on a sheet of fruit leather. Roll, chill, and slice with a very sharp knife. If there is any left after serving, store in freezer.

ROSE HIPS

THERE IS MORE THAN JUST BEAUTY IN A WILD ROSE. THE LITTLE BERRY that follows the blossoms and gives added beauty to our fall foliage has health value too. It is one of the richest known sources of vitamin C. Three average rose hips contain as much vitamin C as one medium-sized orange. Rose hips have a property that prevents loss of vitamin C during cooking, canning or drying.

Collecting ROSE HIPS

IDA WEGELIN

THERE ARE DIFFERENT TYPES OF ROSE HIPS. THE BEST ONES ARE THOSE that are soft when you pick them and are usually a dark, almost maroon-red colour. You'll find that the somewhat elongated hips are very good. The bright red, firm hips don't yield a great deal of pulp for the amount of work in collecting and de-tailing them.

During my childhood—Depression years—money was tight so we spent many hours collecting wild fruits, rose hips being one of them. My mother made lots of rose hip jam. She also made rose hip ketchup. In making ketchup, the spices are important so she used a tomato ketchup recipe as a base and substituted rose hip pulp in place of tomatoes.

Ways to use Rose Hips
Once you have tried rose hips you will find that there are many ways to use them in foods served on the daily menu.
1. Rose hip purée or syrup, fresh or canned, can be used in baked products such as bread, buns, biscuits, drop cookies, cake and gingerbread. Add 50 mL (¼ c) of purée to recipe. It may be necessary to reduce the liquid a little except in muffins. If using juice or syrup, use about 30 mL (2 tbsp) or more to replace equal amount of liquid in recipe. The flavour will not be noticed in foods with distinct flavours such as spice

or molasses, but not so suitable for more delicate-flavoured cakes or cookies.

2. Rose hip purée can be added to desserts such as ice cream or fruit whip. Up to 90–120 mL (6–8 tbsp) can be added to a batch of ice cream without the flavour being discerned.

3. Rose hip purée or syrup can be added to soups. Try adding 15–30 mL (1–2 tbsp) to potato or vegetable soup.

4. To make an excellent spread for toast, muffins or hot cakes, combine 1 part rose hip purée to 3 parts honey.

5. Simply pick raw hips and eat or serve seeded and chopped or cut in halves, in salads or sandwich fillings. Be sure to remove seeds and most of the hairs as they are irritating to the digestive tract.

6. Rose hip purée can be used in sandwich fillings combined with cheese, canned salmon, peanut butter, etc.

DRIED Rose Hips

Cut in halves lengthwise and dry in warm oven, turning occasionally. Be careful not to overheat or they will turn brown in colour. When properly dried they are a distinct red colour. They can also be dried in a food dehydrator. When dry, remove hairs and seeds by shaking in a corn popper or two sieves tied together. A fan helps to blow out hairs. Store in covered jars in a dry place. To use, soak and boil in water until consistency of purée or tomato sauce. Use as purée. The dried hips can also be used to make a tea.

ROSE HIP & Apple Juice Cocktail

15 mL (1 tbsp)	rose hip purée
5 mL (1 tsp)	honey
500 mL (2 c)	apple juice

Mix rose hip purée and honey. Stir mixture into chilled apple juice.

Rose Hip CATSUP

4 L (4 qt)	ripe rose hips
2	medium-sized onions
1	clove garlic
250 mL (1 c)	water (more if necessary)

Boil ingredients until they are soft. Strain.

180 mL (¾ c)	brown sugar

Add brown sugar. Tie in bag and add:

7 mL (½ tbsp)	whole allspice
7 mL (½ tbsp)	whole mace
7 mL (½ tbsp)	whole cloves
7 mL (½ tbsp)	celery seed
5 cm (2 in)	stick cinnamon

Boil these ingredients quickly. Add:

250 mL (1 c)	vinegar
to taste	cayenne
	salt (optional)

Boil catsup 10 minutes longer. Bottle at once in sterilized jars or bottles. Seal bottles with wax. The flavour of the catsup is excellent.

Rose Hip JAM

IDA WEGELIN

Wash 1 L (4 c) of fully ripe, frost-nipped rose hips and place in 500 mL (2 c) of boiling water. Boil gently until soft, mash with wooden spoon and strain through a jelly bag overnight. Measure juice and water up to 750 mL (3 c). Wash and cut up 1 kg (¾ lb) of green apples. Cook gently to a pulp, then rub through a sieve. Mix rose hip juice and apple pulp, bring to a boil. Stir in 1 kg (4 c) sugar. When dissolved boil rapidly to jelly stage. Put in hot sterilized jars and seal.

Rose Hip & FRUIT JELLY

Use rose hips that are green or semi-ripe, as ripe hips have very little pectin. A better jelly is obtained if commercial pectin is used. A batch of jelly will take about ½ package crystal pectin. Jellies made with all or part honey seem to have a better flavour. A little acid, such as lemon juice, adds to the flavour. Most rose hip products will be softer at first but will stiffen on standing. Do not place in sun to stiffen as this destroys vitamin C.

Rose Hip & CRABAPPLE JELLY

Use half crabapple juice and half rose hip purée. To 250 mL (1 c) of this mixture, use 180 mL (¾ c) sugar or honey. Less rose purée may be used, such as 1 part purée to 3 parts crabapple, if flavour of rose hip is not desired.

ROSE HIP &
Other Fruit Jelly & Jam

Rose hip purée may be combined in jelly and jam with fruit such as cranberry, grape, chokecherry, red currant, etc. Combine 1 part rose hip purée to 2 parts fruit or 1:3 if rose hip flavour is not desired. Honey and lemon add to flavour.

CANNED Rose Hip Purée

Wash hips, remove stems and hull. Put through food chopper using medium knife. Cover completely with water and simmer until quite tender (about 5 minutes). Press through sieve. Can without sugar by processing in pint sealers for 30 minutes or add 125 mL (½ c) sugar or honey to each 250 mL (1 c) of purée. Boil 5 minutes and bottle in sterilized jars.

ABC Sandwich Filling

This is a very nutritious sandwich; the carrots provide vitamin A, the wheat germ, B vitamins and the rose hip purée, vitamin C. The honey adds energy and makes it taste good. It is particularly good on rye or whole wheat bread.

15 mL (1 tbsp) honey	Combine ingredients, adding sufficient wheat germ to thicken the mixture to sandwich-spread consistency.
5 mL (1 tsp) rose hip purée	
1 small carrot, grated	
wheat germ	

ROSE HIP Syrup

Wash hips, remove stems and hull. Put through food chopper using medium knife. Cover completely with 1½ L (3 pt) boiling water to 1 kg (2 lb) hips and boil for 2 minutes. Using a sieve, run as much liquid through as can be put through without effort. Drain remainder using jelly bag or 2 thicknesses of fine cheesecloth. Measure liquid (should be 750 mL/1½ pt). If more, boil down. This juice may be bottled and processed for 15 minutes without sugar, although upon opening, it does not keep as long as with sugar.

To make syrup: Add 180 mL (¾ c) sugar (or less), boil 5 minutes. Bottle in hot sterilized sealers or small bottles and process 10 minutes. Using small bottles that do not seal, such as vanilla, dip top of bottle in paraffin wax immediately upon removing from water bath.

Canned Whole ROSE HIPS

Wash hips, stem and hull. To save time during the busy canning season, these may be canned whole. Pack in sealer to within 1 cm (½ in) of top, cover with hot water and process for 30 minutes. To use later: Press through sieve and strain through cheesecloth. Use as purée or just drain in jelly bag and use as juice or syrup.

Recipe INDEX

NOTES